on track ...
Soft Machine

every album, every song

Scott Meze

sonicbondpublishing.com

Sonicbond Publishing Limited
www.sonicbondpublishing.co.uk
Email: info@sonicbondpublishing.co.uk

First Published in the United Kingdom 2023
First Published in the United States 2023

British Library Cataloguing in Publication Data:
A Catalogue record for this book is available from the British Library

Typeset in ITC Garamond Std & ITC Avant Garde Gothic
Printed and bound in England

Graphic design and typesetting: Full Moon Media

Follow us on social media:
Twitter: https://twitter.com/SonicbondP
Instagram: www.instagram.com/sonicbondpublishing_/
Facebook: www.facebook.com/SonicbondPublishing/

Linktree QR code:

on track ...
Soft
Machine

every album, every song

Scott Meze

sonicbondpublishing.com

on track ...

Soft Machine

Contents

Introduction

This book documents one of the most fascinating stories in rock. It constitutes a checklist of the essential discography for Soft Machine and their offshoots and a selection of albums representing the most relevant of the extracurricular careers of their key personnel. For retrospective live and compilation albums, it lists current best-in-class releases. Around the 19 featured albums it wraps a detailed biographical framework mainly to aid exploration: the available live and session materials by the same line-up, and the solo works you might be interested in.

Before we start, let's admit it: Soft Machine are a beast of a band. Just on personnel alone, they're monstrously complicated to assimilate. A decade after their formation in 1966, they had no original members left, and none of those original members have ever re-joined. At that point, the group became a state of mind, and yet defining what made them unique – a centre of gravity that meant they were still a recognizable entity regardless of who was actually performing – had become impossible long before then. With other resilient but constantly churning bands of the period, such as Fairport Convention, Deep Purple, or Yes, the listener can map out the group's eras, creating a band narrative from each permutation and advance. That's not possible here. Soft Machine seem somehow to blend together over the years, and their albums – all obstinately numbered up to 1973's *Seven* – do not represent a progression in the traditional sense.

Pete Frame's attempt to organise the band's history in January 1977, a messy sheet created for the *Triple Echo* compilation, produced a densely plotted family tree that was as difficult to comprehend as the band themselves, weirdly unfocused, and still only selective. Frame listed 15 line-ups, and his tree omits the various offshoots and diversions that see ever-permeating diffractions of what they made possible. But how could he cram it all on? Soft Machine are an incredibly connective band. You can draw direct lines between them and a wide swathe of British music in the 1960s and beyond.

Some connections are simple enough. Softs member Kevin Ayers leads to Mike Oldfield, Daevid Allen to Steve Hillage, Mark Charig to Robert Fripp. Others are surprising leaps sideways. Ric Sanders went on to become a stalwart of Fairport Convention. Dave MacRae worked with Cass Elliot, Olivia Newton-John, and the Goodies. Alan Wakeman was a long-term sideman for David Essex. Andy Summers, another direct link to Fripp, was of course, a global teen pinup with The Police.

In the incestuous annals of British sessions and fluid band membership, we can also link Soft Machine directly to artists as diverse as Jimi Hendrix, Eric Burdon, Jon Lord, Humble Pie, Manfred Mann, Henry Cow, John Martyn, Nick Drake, Brian Eno, Jack Bruce, Elton John, Bert Jansch, Steve Hackett, and Arthur Brown – that's the pop, blues, folk, prog, and avant-garde scenes right there, and it's just the start. Want a hotline between Roy Harper and

Uriah Heep? Look no further. Nico and Pink Floyd? One easy step. With 27 official members and a further nine in offshoot bands with a 'Soft' in their name, Soft Machine seem to be right in the thick of it. And I haven't even mentioned the tangled skeins of the Canterbury Scene, the much wider British jazz-fusion scene to which they are central and essential, the array of European players that saw Soft Machine as an ongoing cultural focus and awkward progenitor, and the host of recent bands across the world that have refracted and reinvented their sound.

And yet, let's go out on the street now and talk to girls in short skirts. Those who aren't beating you back with their Michael Kors handbags are giving you blank stares, and so, I bet, are the majority of their brothers. Soft Machine remain largely unknown in their native Britain, and they never quite cracked America. Save for one blip in 1970/1971 that saw *Third* and *Fourth* nudge the British charts, their sales were always meagre, and the original band's career barely remained afloat for the 13 years it lasted. But within the niche of their sound world, their stature remains immense. I bet there's not an issue of *Prog* magazine today in which someone doesn't acknowledge their influence.

If the wider world has very little understanding of who Soft Machine are and what they mean, it's largely the band's own fault. No other artist in the history of rock has been as pig-headed. During their entire initial run, they eschewed making emotional connection on stage. They didn't care what people thought of them, they had no interest in compromising to meet commercial values, and they made no effort to lower themselves to the masses. They seemed purposefully designed to be unapproachable and aloof to newcomers, with a sound to which you had to accommodate yourself rather than expect anything resembling a learning curve. Venture into the hall where they were booked in 1970, and you were likely to hear half-hour-long pieces divested of comprehensible structure and played at brain-splitting volume intended to drive you back out into the street. The band themselves wore earplugs.

Soft Machine were named – as a direct provocation – after William Burroughs's novel, a catalogue of sex fantasies and body horror, but they never claimed outlaw status for bedsit rebels who thought swearing or drug references were the height of transgression. They soon abandoned the conventional games of pop, meaning no hit singles to lodge in your head, no youth anthems, no inviting melodies to hum, precious few songs of any kind, and little of the traditional virtuosity where you can fixate on a musician's skills as a handle on the larger construct. Even their best seller *Third* attempts to distance you from the title onwards. It's a plain-wrapped, hermetically sealed double album with one track per side, and you're not going to make the least sense of it until you've struggled to play it many times over. Any failure to penetrate the disc must be yours alone. The band won't help. Open the gatefold and all you see is disdain.

If that's not enough to make the early band seem snooty and unpleasant, there's the way they baited and then derided the so-called highbrow, whose defences were finally tumbling in the late 1960s. All four group members who first brought the name to media attention in 1966 were from well-off families and attended private schools. Keyboard player Mike Ratledge was an Oxford graduate with classical training. The others – guitarist Allen, bassist Ayers, and drummer Robert Wyatt – thought nothing of hopping around Europe and sunning themselves on Mediterranean islands for months. They had family connections. They believed that a band of intelligent radicals could storm a business as idiotic and piecemeal as pop: one-eyed visionaries in the land of the blind.

They were right. Within six months, they were the coolest band in Britain – or the second-coolest, depending on how you view Syd Barrett's similarly haughty Pink Floyd. In the Summer of Love, Soft Machine took their theatre of contempt to the French Riviera, where a hipper-than-London glitterati fawned over hour-long performances of 'We Did It Again' – a piece that was minimal, monotonous, and meant to menace attendees. The avant-garde thought them delectable.

Of course, the unique times helped, but the band couldn't have done it without substance behind them. Like Pink Floyd, Soft Machine were the vanguard of a new kind of sophisticated progressive rock that soon wrested fashion away from smiling bands in matching suits and leering men in their 20s hocking teenage highs. Art schools and the air of betterment, hallucinogenic drugs and the opening of mental horizons, and a new permissive attitude all fed into the remarkable luck that Soft Machine were the right band at the right time.

Before Miles Davis's *Bitches Brew*, before Frank Zappa's *Hot Rats* even, they collided rock, soul, and jazz, concocting a tumbling free-form fusion that was richly psychedelic and thoroughly unpredictable – intensely plotted compositions in complex meters one minute, breakneck improvisations the next. By *Third,* they were the most adventurous of all the progressive bands, pooling into their mix everything from Stockhausen's radical European skronk to Terry Riley's American minimalism. And just like the hip in France, the British establishment bent backwards to accommodate them. They were the first rock band to take their cacophony to the classical stage at the Proms, and they refused to temper the onslaught even for an audience in formal dress.

The result was the expected howl of outrage from snobs threatened by barbarians at the gate – and well they should be, since history showed the barbarians soon overran everything the snobs thought they had secreted away for themselves. But after the Proms, Soft Machine declared they were having none of it. They claimed they didn't like the audience, the attention, or the prestige, and would go back to blowing for longhairs in rock venues, thanks all the same.

9

But it was a smokescreen. The fact is that in 1970, Soft Machine were less-suited to shift into the cultural establishment than Deep Purple. The obstinate nature of their sound precluded widespread acceptance. The Nice had an act just as extreme, but Keith Emerson wrote classical themes for classical instruments, and the last thing Soft Machine were going to do in 1970 was play with an orchestra. Even if the others had thought they could temper their approach to court the market, Soft Machine were hamstrung by a drummer who played topless, thrashed at his kit, and interrupted proceedings for gabbled vocal improvisations. By the time they were rid of him in 1971, their moment had passed.

Yet the exact moment Soft Machine kicked Robert Wyatt off his drum stool is now seen, equally by fans themselves and rock commentators, as the point at which the band lost their edge. Subsequently, the story goes, they became ever more conventional, ever more classical, ever more establishment. They did finally become orchestrated, but only after the band was over. What was lost along the way was a spirit of fearless abandon, which never returned in the 1970s incarnations or in the bulk of the revivals documented at the end of this book.

Arguably, the failure was built into the band from the start. Soft Machine straddled an uncomfortable mid-point between traditional pop groups, which are usually founded around colleagues or friends, and the *ad hoc* aggregations of jazz in which personnel were grafted on for each project in hand – an album, a tour, even a sonic experiment.

The earliest incarnation brought together three ebullient, colourful rock-stars-in-waiting in the form of Allen, Ayers, and Wyatt, all of whom graduated to lead bands of their own. These three men seem to be the heart of Soft Machine, and the closest we get to the charismatic, interview-friendly, media-savvy, game-playing type of band on which pop and rock had flourished since those poster-boy days of – (trot out the names with me) – John, Paul, George, and Ringo.

But the lowbrow/highbrow divide *within the band itself* was both energiser and destabiliser. The prime driver for the band's radicalism in the early days was Daevid Allen, a man whose visionary ambitions butted unfortunately against his lack of proficiency as guitarist and songwriter. Ayers and Wyatt were interested in punctuating the weirdness with bright, relatable songs. Ratledge wanted to concentrate on a harder, more intricate form of electric bebop.

These tensions soon split the band into factions. Allen was out before they'd even recorded an album. The others could have replaced him with a dominant talent to anchor the project. You could reel off the names in late 1967: everybody from Steve Howe to Jimmy Page. With a stretch of the imagination, it could have been band-friend Jimi Hendrix, with whom they shared management, or Syd Barrett. Soft Machine could have been the band that nabbed David Gilmour. Imagine *that* future. Instead, they remained unanchored, undergoing constant upheaval that repeatedly tore the project apart. Ayers quit in 1968, and with Wyatt's ousting it became hard to determine the group's vision at all.

By then, the survivors were relieved simply to have something resembling stability for a few more weeks of hard work for little reward, but the churn never ceased. The closest Soft Machine had to a continuity was Mike Ratledge, a man whose stern public demeanour makes Can's Irmin Schmidt seem cuddly. Ratledge's whole image was distancing, including his decision to balance a strong square jaw with square dark glasses and – bizarrely – to wear them *over* his square-cut hair: a different planet's concept of cool. The media's reaction was dutifully standoffish. If you were to shove Mike Ratledge and Roger Waters into a children's party and lock the door, the inference goes, Waters would be the one making the balloon animals. Ratledge would sit in a corner with a pin.

But even this was feigned. Ratledge was actually a romantic who wrote some of the most lovely compositions in all jazz-fusion. He simply never tried to play rock star. No wizard's cape for him, no humping the Hammond back and forth. He wanted only the *music* to matter, and the music he made remained vital and distinctive all the way up to his own departure in 1976.

Bewildered? Let's summarise so far. An unfathomable cast of players. Progression that is not progress. A state of mind it's impossible to define. Rock's formative lowbrow/highbrow argument. An icehouse image for a band yearning for communication. Band newbies, you have your work cut out for you.

And that's where I hope I can help. In this book, I'll make Soft Machine hospitable, show that the recorded works are all welcoming and navigable, and reveal the human behind the machine.

Where to start the story is simple – with the band's origins, apprenticeships, and long gestation. Where to end it is much harder. To date, 13 studio albums (including *Third* and *Alive And Well Recorded In Paris*, which saw studio work to enhance live material) have been released under the Soft Machine brand. But the most recent of these – *Hidden Details* (2018) and *Other Doors* (2023) – qualify only because the offshoot group Soft Machine Legacy decided to drop one word from their name. *Land Of Cockayne* (1981) has even less claim to being a *true* Soft Machine album, since it was a posthumous studio construct using only a few then-recent members and a host of session musicians. Bear in mind that some snifflers claim the only legitimate iterations of Soft Machine are those containing Ratledge (or Wyatt or Ayers or Allen: take your pick). As I write this, the earliest-joining member of the current Soft Machine came to the group in 1975. The next-earliest joined 40 years later.

I decided to include all the studio albums by groups with a 'Soft' in their name that include members who were in Soft Machine at any point in the 1970s – including revival groups that try in ways large and small to continue the parent band's legacy, but excluding tribute bands and projects. I incorporate bands such as Soft Works, Soft Bounds, and Soft Machine Legacy, even if recent iterations are far removed from the 1970s band (let alone the 1960s version) in sound, attitude, and temperament. The Legacy version even talk and smile on stage, the rotters.

So let's begin with one young man's arrival in the UK in 1960. He doesn't know what he's going to find there, but he does know he's going to blow up a storm.

The Roots Of The Canterbury Scene

Britain in 1960 seems prehistoric to us now. There was no music save the bellowing of old men in public houses, a little homemade skiffle and trad jazz, and the greasy finger-snapping of teddy boys chasing a lifestyle an ocean away in that void long after the bulk of the American servicemen had gone home. Many of those who would form the heart of the prog rock revolution were still in short trousers. But things *were* moving in this grim grey past. Five kids, scruffy in their teenage leathers, were heading off to Hamburg and the unimaginable that awaited them there. The leader, John Lennon, was 19 years old and thought he knew everything. The youngest, George Harrison, was 17 and knew he knew nothing. The authorities would kick The Beatles out of West Germany when they discovered Harrison's age, but they'd be back. With retrospect, how closely it seems their paths crossed with an Australian musician heading in the opposite direction on the long voyage of betterment that would eventually lead him, if only for a short time, to Soft Machine.

That you probably immediately thought of Daevid Allen shows how deeply Allen has embedded into those days of far-off legend. But actually, Allen was only one of two future Softs to make the journey from Australia to Britain in 1960. Ray Warleigh (like Allen, born in 1938) preceded him by several months, and unlike Allen, who struggled for years to establish himself, was soon embedded in the London jazz and R&B scene, working with everyone from Humphrey Lyttleton to Alexis Korner.

Allen scuffled in and out of England, France, and Spain for years on what was at least partly his parents' largesse, somehow networking his way into the company of scene makers in all those places, and pushing his rudimentary guitar playing into the one forum where prowess mattered the least: the embryonic free-jazz and performance-poetry scene.

The first of these sojourns was propitious indeed. At the end of 1960, Allen found lodging in the village of Lydden in Kent, staying with the Ellidge family, which included 15-year-old son Robert. (Robert Wyatt-Ellidge seems to have used the name Ellidge up to 1967, as that is how he was credited on his side of the first Soft Machine single 'Feelin' Reelin' Squeelin''. He changed it to his mother's name Wyatt thereafter. This book follows suit.)

Allen brought into the house a collection of avant-garde jazz albums and a carefully cultivated dope-smoking beatnik attitude. This made the 22-year-old a figure of cool to Robert and his fellows, which included the brothers Brian and Hugh Hopper, Mike Ratledge, and Dave Sinclair, all of whom attended Simon Langton Grammar School For Boys about ten miles away in Canterbury. Also circling this scene was rapscallion native Kevin Ayers, who'd been posted back down to Kent by his mother after scrapes in London involving squatting, begging, and drugs that got the boy a stay in borstal. The plan was to keep him out of bad company.

A shared love of music led to various permutations of performance and songwriting but nothing that might yet be considered remarkable compared

13

to the thousands of other British boys who were also teaching themselves to play and act cool (and smoke a joint or two) in this immediate pre-Beatles period. Ellidge learned drums, trumpet, and violin. Ayers gravitated to the guitar, and Hugh Hopper to the bass. Ratledge – pretty much the star of the school, and soon to head up to Oxford to study psychology – was a classically trained pianist. Clarinettist Brian Hopper had also had classical training but became enamoured of the electric guitar as played by slippy-spectacled Hank Marvin of 'Apache' fame.

Just as significant as Allen's arrival were the links the Ellidges had to poet and author Robert Graves, then in his mid-60s. Graves lived in the village of Deià on the Spanish island of Mallorca, which was then undergoing an artistic flowering based as much on an influx of psychedelic drugs as Graves himself. These links took Allen and Ayers to Deià, and both men later spent long periods living there.

Over the following years, as Allen wove in and out of the frame, the budding musicians collided, experimented, and laid the foundations for their careers to come. Some of their home-taped dabblings were released in 1998 on the four volumes of *Canterburied Sounds* (repackaged as a four-disc set in 2013) curated by Hugh Hopper, and a few even made it to the 2001 Softs compilation *Man In A Deaf Corner*. Little of this work is of interest to anybody except the Soft Machine completist, but it does show a steady shift in emphasis from rock'n'roll standards to jazz blowing. By 1963, Allen, Hugh Hopper, and Ellidge – on guitar, bass, and drums respectively – were able to try their hand in London as a free-jazz act called The Daevid Allen Trio, which occasionally roped in a visiting Ratledge on piano. They managed stints at Peter Cook's Establishment Club, the Marquee Club, and even The Institute Of Contemporary Arts alongside William Burroughs.

A recording of one of the quartet's performances at the Marquee survives, and was released in 1993 as *Live 1963*. How well you handle this first Softs-related salvo depends on whether or not you can cope with Allen's affectation of the time, which was to recite his poor-man's Beat rhyme in a studiously lifeless and condescending drawl. There's no actual singing, though he does modulate his voice during 'Capacity Travel'. It's the nadir of the set. There's nothing in Hopper's plunking bass or Ellidge's rudimentary drumming to suggest they'd ever make the grade, nor that backing Allen in jazz clubs was a route forward. Allen's inept guitar work puts the lie to his claim that 1967's *Jet Propelled Photographs* merely caught him off-form. Ratledge sits in on the freeform centrepiece 'Dear Old Benny Green Is A-Turning In His Grave' and does at least lash the excursion to the band's Ornette Coleman and Cecil Taylor pretensions, but Allen's guitar remains the sonic focus.

In short, the band couldn't have survived long. They were either too radical or too awful. In the event, Allen followed Burroughs to Paris in the autumn, sundering the relationship. There Allen dropped LSD, sold dope, and circulated with other movers in the scene – most notably Terry Riley, who was working on what would become 'In C'. The two men performed together, at one point amplifying the sounds of their scooters on stage. This was a trick Allen's Soft Machine would repeat on at least two occasions – the *International Times* launch party in October 1966 and the 14 Hour Technicolor Dream in April 1967.

Riley was the most important of Allen's contacts, if only because it was Riley who introduced Allen to tape-loop techniques. When Hugh Hopper came to visit in 1964, he too became obsessed with loops, and was soon a master at splicing tape compositions. Allen's solo performances consisted of him reciting his poems to a tape backing seemingly mostly created from Hopper's loops. The style led to Allen's most important early work, an extraordinary 30-minute collage created for the BBC in 1965 (broadcast in 1967) called 'The Switch Doctor', which we can assume must have been much how one of these performances sounded. The piece was released on the 1993 CD version of *The Death Of Rock & Other Entrances*. Further loop constructs litter his post-Softs work, both solo and with Gong.

Some of Hopper's tape manipulations for Soft Machine were released on *Third* and *Spaced* (1996), and other pieces formed the basis of his solo albums, such as *1984* (1973). Even Robert Wyatt had loop compositions on *Third* and his solo album *The End Of An Ear* (1970). Indeed, for that period surrounding *Third*, tape manipulation was a Soft Machine characteristic.

Allen seems to have spent very little time in the UK after 1963. Eventually, he migrated down to Deià where he remained until 1966 – dropping more acid, soaking up the sun, and somehow surviving on doing nothing much at all. Without him, Ellidge and Hopper returned to Canterbury. In the autumn of 1964, Ratledge returned to university and the other players formed a new band: The Wilde Flowers. They consisted of Ayers on vocals, Brian Hopper on lead guitar, Hugh Hopper on bass, Ellidge on drums, and Dave Sinclair's cousin Richard on rhythm guitar. A careful shift from experimental jazz to a more-acceptable mix of pop, soul, and R&B gained them a following in the – let's admit it, somewhat provincial – Canterbury teen dance scene, and slowly their abilities and their reach expanded.

Given that this band would eventually become Caravan, the most commercial of the Canterbury Scene bands, it's possible to make a case that much of this chapter is irrelevant to that scene – in other words, that Allen (who was never a Wilde Flowers member and doesn't appear *at all* on *Canterburied Sounds*) may have helped kick-start the ambitions of these young players but had little direct influence on their mature sound, as would also be true with Soft Machine.

As well as the teenybopper hits, The Wilde Flowers peppered their sets with the odd jazz excursion – though never radically enough to prevent the kids on the dance floor swinging their arms from side to side – and even a few self-penned songs. They also hit on two innovations that would follow into The Soft Machine. Ellidge seems occasionally to have performed without a shirt, something he claimed was a necessity since he sweated so much but which garnered him welcome notice from the girls on the floor. The other innovation was to segue their songs – either directly or with linking passages – so that the rhythm never ended and the dancing never ceased. This was genuinely new. Only a few soul groups were attempting anything remotely similar and not nearly to such an extent. Certainly, we were still some way off pop and rock albums where the songs ran together, and in 1965, even The Grateful Dead and The Mothers Of Invention weren't doing the same, even if The Wilde Flowers could have heard of them.

In 1965, Ayers decided he'd rather be in Deià than poking around half-filled dance floors in Canterbury, and absconded to the Med. After a short period with replacement vocalist Graham Flight, The Wilde Flowers nudged Ellidge to the microphone, necessitating the recruitment of a new drummer, Richard Coughlan. Sinclair *also* quit in 1965, but little by little it is Caravan that is melding here, and the Caravan sound that is sliding into focus.

The Wilde Flowers left behind no contemporary releases, but a scattered residue of demos and other amateur recordings have been issued on an untitled 1994 CD. From a session by the original five-piece at Wout Steenhuis's home studio in Broadstairs on the tip of Kent, attributed to March 1965, we have our first two notable original compositions: Ayers singing endearingly out of key on 'She's Gone' and an instrumental version of what was to become 'Memories'. A tape dated only to summer or autumn that year bequeathed us three tracks with Flight on vocals, and they're all originals – Hugh's 'Don't Try To Change Me', Brian's 'Slow Walkin' Talk', and Ellidge's 'He's Bad For You'. A fourth recording from the period sees Richard Sinclair at the microphone for Hugh's 'It's What I Feel', which was later rerecorded as 'A Certain Kind' for the first Soft Machine album. Sinclair's voice, as pleasingly lugubrious as Ringo Starr's, may have inspired Ayers to sing the same way.

The final session of the period, dated to spring 1966, has the four-piece Coughlan band back in Broadstairs for another set of originals, mostly written by Hugh. 'Memories' now has a plaintive Ellidge vocal, 'Never Leave Me' leans toward the strident pop of 'Love Makes Sweet Music', and 'Impotence' presages Wyatt's confessional lyrics on the first three Soft Machine albums.

The Daevid Allen Soft Machine

Having quit The Wilde Flowers, Ayers arrived on Mallorca for what he thought would be a long period of indolence. He came armed with the latest UK hits. Among the discs was The Yardbirds' 'Evil Hearted You'/'Still I'm Sad', produced by Giorgio Gomelsky. The latter song caught Allen's ear. A simple blues dirge, it featured a slurred and strangely inflected lead vocal over a moody accompaniment meant to sound like a Gregorian choir. Significantly, there were no Jeff Beck pyrotechnics at all.

As Allen's self-mythology told it later, 'Still I'm Sad' convinced him that pop was finally up to his standards, or down to his abilities, depending on how deeply you read between the lines. He believed either that pop now had the sophistication of proper music and hence was worthy of his attention, or reckoned that it was now so free a church that even a maverick non-player like himself stood a chance.

Either way, fame beckoned a second time. He and Ayers began writing songs with the idea that they'd form a band and play stadiums just like The Beatles. The idea would likely have remained a pipe dream – at the time Mallorca was, after all, a geographically isolated Mediterranean island with no chance of building up a significant following – except in April 1966 Ayers encountered Wes Brunson, an American businessman vacationing in Deià. Ayers plied Brunson with LSD and sold him, goggle-eyed, on the idea of divesting his optometry business and using the money to finance a pop group that would conquer the world. Specifically, the pop group that Ayers and Allen would build around themselves, on rhythm guitar and bass respectively, with American island-hopper Larry Nowlin on lead.

Armed with the promise of Brunson's cash, the three hot-footed to Canterbury and began approaching old colleagues to fill the gaps. Hugh Hopper laughed them off, but Ellidge was willing to hedge his bets by alternating his Wilde Flowers gigs with playing drums and singing for the new group. Ellidge brought with him a missing half of their live set, which consisted of the cream of his other band's songs.

True to his word, Brunson arrived in May, buying them gear and a place to live and paying their wages. Allen named the group Mr. Head, which was hardly going to go down a riot among the teenyboppers but was significantly better than The Bishops Of Canterbury or Dingo Virgin And The Four Skins. They managed a handful of gigs in June before their wannabe-Brian-Epstein suffered a meltdown and was carted off back to the US, stopping their funds dead.

Geared up and with a set to sell, they decided to try their luck in London. There Nowlin managed to achieve his solitary useful service for the group – he gained a connection to Mike Jeffrey and Chas Chandler, who'd started a pop management business called Anim and were on the lookout for talent. They didn't seem impressed by Mr. Head, but decided that Ayers's songs had promise and knew they'd need writers for whatever *serious* artists they found. In the event, the artist they found was Jimi Hendrix – soon to show himself adept at writing his own material – but by then, Ayers had a foot in Anim's door. Jeffrey and Chandler took on the band with a wage and they settled down to hunt for work.

By this point, with Cream not yet launched and The Beatles' *Revolver* not yet released, guitar groups seemed to be on the way out. The bands on the R&B circuit (The Graham Bond Organisation, The Spencer Davis Group, Manfred Mann, The Moody Blues, etc.) all had organs to swell their sound. Mr. Head needed one too. Luckily, Ratledge was now a graduate and had just come back from a trip to New York, where he'd hung out in jazz clubs and found himself in William Burroughs's orbit. He was even amenable to join, which is baffling since he had no interest in pop. Presumably, Allen's enthusiasm rubbed off on him. Allen's presence already made the band distinctly schizophrenic, veering from straight songs to freeform improvisations, performance poetry, and the avant-garde. If the pop business could accommodate this, then surely it could also accommodate Ratledge's jazz and classical leanings. The group was also something to do that didn't involve proper work, a means of buying time while he built up his credentials and contacts as *serious* musician and composer (this *serious* not being the same as the *Anim* serious), and a way to meet people and score girls, and the band offered to buy him that all-important and expensive tool of the trade, an instrument of his own.

Unfortunately, there wasn't the Hammond he craved. All they could afford was a Vox Continental – a sort of transistorised briefcase on stilts. (John Lennon had famously elbowed one at Shea Stadium.) It had keys, so it was half way there. Ratledge settled down to comping soul changes on stage with the group. By his own admission, he didn't write anything or even take the role that seriously until Allen's departure.

The richer sound required a relaunch, so Ayers rechristened them The Soft Machine – something of a shoo-in given that now two members had Burroughs connections. (The definite article disappeared around the band's second album, which is where this book dispenses with it, too.)

My suspicion is, Ratledge's presence notwithstanding, that The Soft Machine thought of themselves primarily as a pop group. They wanted to be rich and famous. They wanted to have hits, to be on *Top Of The Pops*, and command pinup features in *Jackie* magazine. Like a band they closely resembled in outlook in mid-1966, The Pink Floyd (also soon to drop their definite article), they were far too wayward to manage it in straight terms as a Beatles-style wall of smiling young lads whom the girls would swoon over, even if Ellidge did take his shirt off at every opportunity. Like The Pink Floyd, their musicians veered from a competent, classically trained keyboard player to a bassist who could hardly play his instrument. They, too, were forced to compensate for the inadequacies of the group by filling their sets with excursions into tweaky noises and weird happenings.

In other words, it's wrong to think of The Soft Machine as an intellectual jazz band in waiting. They were actually the most radical soul group of their day. They continued to aspire to pop hits throughout their first two years, and to write songs into 1969. After they'd each left the group, Allen, Ayers, and Wyatt persisted in writing commercial songs and chasing hits, though in the event only Wyatt actually managed them. Ayers's singles were terrific but surprisingly overlooked. Allen's were uniformly awful. At least until 1970, Soft Machine didn't edge out their commercial material so much as have it robbed from them with the departure of two of their songwriters. By that point, the emerging progressive rock market had shifted the baseline for bands like Soft Machine and Pink Floyd and hits were no longer required. It was only then that both bands ceased attempting them.

In the meantime, a disastrous residency at the Star-Club in Hamburg crunched their momentum, and Nowlin was forced out. The others shuffled their instruments, placing Allen on lead guitar and Ayers on bass. The underground rescued them as it had rescued The Pink Floyd. The Soft Machine began to play the same happenings, psychedelic events, and Notting Hill community gigs that the Floyd were playing, including the high-profile launch party for *IT* at the Roundhouse on 15 October. Like The Pink Floyd, too, this folded them into the London counterculture, and they found a home in the forgiving, acid-saturated basement of the UFO club, where Mark Boyle's lightshow brought excitement to their performances and where the improvs and experiments could be as radical as they liked. And finally – just like the Floyd – this welcoming little community was shelter from an uncomprehending outer world that looked on them with cold, uncaring eyes.

They might have made it. After all, The Pink Floyd did. 'Love Makes Sweet Music' – which Ayers had written in Hamburg – showed promise. Producer Kim Fowley asked Anim to give him a shot at recording them, holding sessions in December 1966 and January 1967 at CBS Studios, but decided that Allen's 'Fred The Fish' was the better song. Fowley was the doyen of the novelty single, and likely his thinking was that The Soft Machine, too, could be marketed as freaks.

At this point, Chandler stepped in, told Fowley to take a hike, and ditched 'Fred The Fish' for good. An acetate of the song was wedged without accreditation onto the end of *Live 1963* as 'Frederique La Poisson Avec Frite Sur De Dos'. As an atrocious mock-Australian knees-up (and structurally identical to the version on Allen's 1971 solo album *Banana Moon*) with a muted trumpet solo, it's likely that Fowley thought it could follow Rolf Harris's fame into the charts. We should all be thankful it did not.

Instead, in February, Chandler had the band record 'Love Makes Sweet Music'. It was released the same month on Polydor, beating the Floyd's 'Arnold Layne' into the shops by the better part of a month: hence qualifying as the underground's first artifact.

'Love Makes Sweet Music' (Ayers)

It was certainly a step up from the songs in the previous chapter, but I suspect much of this has to do with the congested production, a densely plotted summation of every soul trick to date – restless, shape-shifting snippets of melody that are not actually hummable, layer upon layer of Ellidge's vocals to ape excitement, Allen's strenuous bass (he's back on the instrument for this session) pushed too high in the mix. You've heard everything in the first 30 seconds, but the disc keeps bludgeoning you as if terrified you might lift the needle off. So you continue, chasing the chimera of a meaningful lyric or a head-clearing instrumental break. The underground hip – which were to detest *The Piper At The Gates Of Dawn* – must have pinched their noses at this, even as they filled the Blarney Club floor to bop wildly to it.

'Feelin' Reelin' Squeelin'' (Ellidge)

The B-side, actually mostly written by Ayers, was a holdover from the Fowley sessions and is much more interesting. Ayers's vocal in the verses is a comedy monster meant to get the little girls shrinking from his saliva-dripping advance into the arms of Ellidge's bright, sunshiny chorus. Somebody twitters manically on a whistle and sings incompetent harmonies, and Ratledge makes shrill noises on the Vox Continental. The freak-out instrumental, when it finally arrives, sounds like a prototype for Second Hand, one of the best – now largely forgotten – bands of the period.

A few backhanders got the disc some play and a showing in some radio charts, but sales were poor. This kind of hype wasn't uncommon in 1967: 'Arnold Layne' was nudged up the listings using the same method.

Around the same time, the band tried to add blues singer Marsha Hunt to the line-up so that Ellidge could concentrate on drums. Hunt's involvement doesn't seem to have involved any gigs, but it again shows that The Soft Machine thought of themselves as an ersatz black soul and R&B group that also span off into weird improvisations centred around Allen's melting pot of influences.

When things started happening for The Pink Floyd, they happened fast. An unknown band playing to a roomful of counterculture freaks in December 1966 had gained an EMI contract in January 1967 and begun sessions for their first album in February. The Soft Machine might have hoped for the same, but they struggled to get noticed by the majors in the wake of the commercial failure of 'Love Makes Sweet Music'. Eventually, Giorgio Gomelsky himself showed interest, and in April, he took the band into De Lane Lea to record a series of publisher demos just in case there was a hit or even an LP hidden up their paisley sleeves. After three days, Anim shut down the sessions again, this time from a financial dispute.

Nine of the ten songs recorded ended up in Gomelsky's hands. The tenth, another version of 'Fred The Fish', has vanished without trace. The nine were

- - - -

first released on the BYG label in 1972 as *Faces And Places Vol. 7*, and have been repackaged repeatedly since, usually as *Jet Propelled Photographs*.

'That's How Much I Need You Now' (Wyatt)
Much later folded into the central section of 'Moon In June', this hesitant soul ballad likely has Wyatt accompanying himself on piano, given how much the instrumental break sounds like his piece 'A Last Straw' from *Rock Bottom*. There are no other players.

'Save Yourself' (Wyatt)
It's a shame this promising song lapses into the same style as 'Feelin' Reelin' Squeelin'', complete with excruciating backing vocals, but at least Ratledge gets a brief – if undistinguished – organ solo. The band thought enough of the piece to revamp it in 1968 for their first album.

'I Should've Known' (Hugh Hopper)
Also on the first album, with an identical structure and a partially revised lyric under the title 'Why Am I So Short?', this seven-and-a-half-minute song is by far the most substantial from the session. It gains the length thanks to a promising instrumental that winds through a series of psychedelic dance-band changes during which Allen dreams of being Jeff Beck. A drum solo with Pink Floyd mouth noises ups the energy at the end.

'Jet-Propelled Photograph' (Ayers)
Yet another song that would be recycled, this one turned up as the title track to Ayers's second solo album *Shooting At The Moon* (1970), greatly transfigured but with identical words and the same head-hurting rhythm. It seems actually to have been called 'I'm So Low'. In no possible alternate dimension could this be considered a potential hit, but it's as enthralling here as it would be in Ayers's hands.

'When I Don't Want You' (Hugh Hopper)
We have Hopper to thank for so much, but surely not this walking blues notable only for a Ratledge organ solo, which realises it has nowhere to go almost directly after its scintillating opening notes.

'Memories' (Hugh Hopper)
Already the third version of the song in this book, 'Memories' eventually had a life of its own outside Soft Machine (who, oddly, never revisited it), including Allen's carbon copy on *Banana Moon* and a host of cover versions. It was also the session's only excerpt released on the 1977 Softs compilation *Triple Echo*. The band doesn't quite know what to do in the breaks, but Wyatt's vocal is as compelling as ever. It remains the best record of the Allen period.

'You Don't Remember' (Wyatt, Allen)

For all his mooted writing sessions in Deià, Allen's legacy with the band is extremely sketchy. He wrote 'Fred The Fish' – and that, apparently, is all, except for this co-write on a song that Wyatt also later incorporated into 'Moon In June' (without an Allen credit). It's the jazziest of the band's tracks, with the makings of a fine groove in the 'but before this feeling dies' refrain that is never quite allowed to develop.

'She's Gone' (Ayers)

A simple pop bounce flavours a song that was surely hopeless commercially but which the band valued enough to attempt again in June. This time, Allen's guitar is in Beck's feedback-speckled acid-rock style.

'I'd Rather Be With You' (Ayers)

It might have been nice for a little more of Ayers in the vocals, but the band thought Wyatt the more attractive singer, even if visually he was all Micky Dolenz to Ayers's Davy Jones. The song has nothing to commend it, and feels somewhat anachronistic for 1967. It's 1965 beat posture topped by an excruciating slowed-down soul coda.

The interesting thing is just how ordinary most of this list is – a set of unimaginative pop songs with the expected lyrics about human relationships. Gomelsky either didn't get around to recording the band's longer, more experimental material or wasn't interested in it. Still, the tape is about ten minutes shy of album length, and the rest might have strayed out into etheric raptures.

Next to give the band a shot was producer Joe Boyd, who took them into Sound Techniques in June, seemingly in the hope of getting some magic down on a single as he'd done with the Floyd. This session has only been released in part. Indeed, we don't even know the extent of what was played. Two Ayers songs – 'Television Dream' and 'What's The Use Of Tryin'' – are supposed to have been recorded now or perhaps earlier in the spring, but they have never surfaced, leaving what on the surface seems to have been the makings of a 45 that Boyd failed to place with a label.

'She's Gone' (Ayers)

A brief piano introduction differentiates this version, after which it's the familiar pop bluster with swells of Vox Continental. The track is as manically crushed into its running time as 'Love Makes Sweet Music', but any steam it works up is hissed away humorously – first for a clunky classical-style piano break with taped William Burroughs interjection, then for a choir of scat, and finally for a rollicking acid guitar solo that collapses into a meltdown.

The piece is hardly a lost treasure, but it had a long release history. It was first on *Triple Echo*, then on *Turns On Volume 1* (2001), and eventually made it to Boyd's autobiography tie-in album *White Bicycles* (2006), in which he claims it *was* released (again on Polydor) but flopped from lack of promotion.

'I Should've Known' (Hugh Hopper)

A strangely diffuse recording on *Turns On Volume 1*, presumably sourced from an acetate, is all we have of the track. Shorn of the long instrumental, the piece has enough momentum to carry it over Allen's guitar solo but seems all revved up with nowhere to go except back around for yet another circuit.

The same month, The Soft Machine were captured at the UFO club on colour film, performing a free improvisation while Allen drawled a poem written for recently imprisoned hash-fiend scene-maker John Hopkins. You can see it on the 2007 DVD *Gong @ Montserrat 1973 And Other Stories*. It's just like 1963 never ended.

With all their failures and disappointments, the band slid into a fractious summer in which they barely held together to endure what gigs they'd managed to secure. The pop impulse – in other words, the means of making money – vied with the jazz-improvisation impulse, which would make none, and everybody fell out with Allen. Not that the uncomprehending audiences cared either way, so the band smothered their boos with a raging torrent of noise, just as a similarly beleaguered Pink Floyd were doing at the same time. The Floyd battered their detractors out of the hall with 'Reaction In G'. The Soft Machine wearied theirs back to the street with interminable renditions of the build-and-release vamp 'We Did It Again'. But you don't gain followers by antagonizing them.

The Soft Machine were trapped by the game. Likely as a result, given that they weren't truly an underground band any more than The Pink Floyd were – they endured the same dichotomy of psychedelic heads (Allen and Ayers) and those that never touched the stuff (Ratledge and Wyatt) – they cultivated an image of cheap-suit art-school quirk, like a prototype Roxy Music, in which the most outré thing you could do for a photo session was stare enigmatically into the distance while holding a silly prop. This was at least better than the post-Allen image, which saw a band modelled on Giles, Giles And Fripp with Ayers in the idiot role.

The essential problem for both The Soft Machine and the Floyd was merely one of timing. 1967 was the last year the industry was mired in its old patterns of pop-fixated, chart-chasing stars and package tours – well, until 1977 brought them all back. For a wholly new band to survive that hostile year, it needed hits. It must also be prepared to perform them in the town halls, pub back-rooms, and workingmen's clubs that masqueraded as a British gigging circuit.

Things *were* changing, but too late to save either band. By mid-1968, an album-based route to survival had been opened by pioneers like The Moody Blues and The Nice. Universities and colleges provided an alternative means to tour, and audiences that actually wanted to listen to exploratory music, and the classical stages opened to bands with ambition. Underground and progressive rock became a force that swiftly commanded as much heft as the singles market. Albums sold more, were more lucrative and desirable, and could keep profits rolling in for years. In less than a decade the struggling and embryonic British bands of 1967 were shifting units by the million and filling stadiums in the US.

Effectively, all The Soft Machine had to do was endure. But I think there's more to their problems than this. Allen was always going to be a limiter, just like how, in the cold light of day, Syd Barrett was a limiter for The Pink Floyd. Allen didn't fit the pattern of adept concert-hall rock bands with serious structures and profound messages. Like Barrett, he was a prescient shock of punk way ahead of its time. But he couldn't have swerved rock's trajectory by himself, way back in 1968, and The Soft Machine likely couldn't have made much headway that year with him in the ranks. The wind was blowing against Allen, even if he couldn't quite sense it for the continental avant-garde set in which the band found temporary solace. With a cold winter closing in, gigs drying up, the counterculture dying fast, and the arty crowd fading away, the rest of the band would surely have soon dropped him at the roadside, just as the Floyd did with their own disrupter.

Either way, the issue appears to have been taken out of their hands. On returning from a long stay in France in September, Allen was turned away in Dover. The story is that he either neglected to apply for the visa that Commonwealth citizens now required to emigrate to Britain or was (again in his own mythology) blacklisted for subversion. His penalty was exclusion from the UK for three years – and of course, the forced quitting from Soft Machine.

Somehow, against all industry odds, Allen carved himself an enduring and highly creative career that did indeed manage to lace the avant-garde throughout. It even included some acceptable guitar work once he'd figured out his two strengths: making a punk squall and stroking the strings to produce a keening noise he dubbed 'glissando'. Both were inspired by Syd Barrett, who in turn had learned them from Keith Rowe of the experimental 1960s group AMM.

Whatever the circumstances of Allen's departure, relations with The Soft Machine remained cordial enough in the early years for the others to stay in touch. France was in thrall of the band, giving Allen the currency to rebuild his base there. He sat in with the others when they visited late in 1967, and was even invited to join them on their 1968 tours of the US – a country to which he *did* still have access. Though he passed on this, he continued to cross paths with Ayers, especially since both men repeatedly retreated to the Balearics for extended vacations.

In 1969, when Ayers told him he was forming his own band, Allen followed suit. From this grew Gong, which played one of its first gigs at the Amougies Festival in November (under the name The Daevid Allen Quartet) on the same stage as Soft Machine. Allen's early sets leaned heavily on Soft Machine material, even including goading audiences with his own renditions of 'We Did It Again'.

His breakout year was 1971. By then, he'd toughened up, gathering a band of spiky players around him for a succession of releases under his own name and the Gong moniker. In February, he joined Hugh Hopper, Robert Wyatt, and Elton Dean on stage at the Roundhouse for a set of solo material and 'Fred The Fish' during a Softs theme night, eventually released in 2012 as *Live At The Roundhouse 1971*. A flavour of emerging Gong played Glastonbury Fayre in June, leading to Allen's superb Softs-style collage 'Glad Stoned Buried Fielding Flash And Fresh Fest Footprints In My Memory' on the memorial triple album *The Electric Score* in 1972. Gong's *Camembert Electrique* was a collision of abrasion and madness including drummer Pip Pyle among its contributors. Pyle was also on board for the band's recording of an album's worth of backing tracks onto which French beat poet Jack-Alain Léger grafted his vocals. The results were released as *Obsolete* by the pseudonymous Dashiell Hedayat. But the most notable release of all was Allen's solo album *Banana Moon*, for which record label BYG requested that at least one other current Soft Machine member be included. In the event, Allen was joined not only by Wyatt but by a past member, Nick Evans, and by Pyle, who would be part of the Softs family in the future. Wyatt sings an excellent version of 'Memories' and Allen camps up his Australian heritage for yet another slapdash version of 'Fred The Fish'. My feeling is that the disk was an attempt to show us all what an Allen Soft Machine should have sounded like if only he'd been allowed to keep cranking its handle.

In the middle of 1971, Ayers again hooked up with Allen, actually joining Gong for about six months. Sadly, there were no studio recordings during this period, but live performances featured a mix of the pair's compositions, including Ayers's song about his sister Kate, 'Clarence In Wonderland'. Ayers then quit to form Decadence, one of whose members was ex-Khan guitarist Steve Hillage. Decadence toured France in December 1972, alerting Allen to the player.

That year, Virgin mail-order LP impresario Richard Branson funded a new record label to bring the better of the European bands to a wider British audience. He left the music in the hands of Simon Draper, a Soft Machine fan who was determined to place as many Canterbury Scene musicians on his roster as he could. Draper snapped up Gong in early 1973. Allen took the opportunity to poach Hillage away from his old friend, after which there were no more Ayers/Allen collaborations.

Of Gong's subsequent torturous history, the Allen albums of note are chiefly the *Radio Gnome Invisible* trilogy recorded for Virgin, consisting of *Flying Teapot* (1973), *Angel's Egg* (1973), and *You* (1974). Many – this writer included – see *Angel's Egg* as Allen's masterpiece, but some Gong members have claimed he contributed less than it appears. He simply slapped vocals across everything and then claimed the credits for himself. This is more obviously true of *You*, in which Allen stopped bothering to join in, and the others picked up the slack by playing long jazzy jams on their own. It is this instrumental work that gained *You* its later reputation as a classic.

The reason Allen disengaged from his own band seems to be a rerun of the Soft Machine debacle. Allen simply wasn't a virtuoso musician. That was fine when he surrounded himself with others who also made a rough-hewn noise and banged about the stage in anarchic happenings. But little by little, Allen had brought adept musicians into the band – those of the stature of Hillage, Mike Howlett, and Pierre Moerlen. The more these players concentrated on their music, the less room there was for Allen's madness. He left the band in April 1975 because he could no longer impose his creative will on it, but the others were likely on the verge of throwing him out anyway. How history turns and turns about.

After 1975, the pickings are patchy, though Allen continued to surprise and at times – such as the Brainville project with Pyle and Hugh Hopper in 1998 – he intersected again with the trajectory of this book. The Brainville catalogue is certainly worth exploring. Completists will also want *Jet Propelled Photographs* (2004) by University Of Errors, in which Allen recreated all those 1967 demos and more, and still didn't put down any guitar to speak of.

The Kevin Ayers Trio

Though there's almost no extant live documentation of the Daevid Allen Soft Machine, we have multiple recordings of the three-piece Soft Machine so soon in the wake of his departure that you can almost hear the background churning of the ferry heading toward France. There are live dates from September and December 1967, and audio from TV and radio sessions. It's as if a cloudy window has just been wiped clean, revealing the band for the first time but also highlighting the extent of our ignorance of what has come before.

In immediate terms, the recordings show a band that had no choice but to continue, as they had obligations in Britain and on the Continent, but also presumably had no time to audition and train a replacement even if they wanted one. The pace of the band's activities in the post-Allen period means they didn't get a chance to break and assess for more than eight months, at which point they did indeed source a new guitarist, Andy Summers. They likely thought the trio was a temporary necessity.

But a lot more happened in those eight months, including a heightened phase of the slow-brooding dichotomy that was eventually to tear the band apart. Allen had been more than just a guitarist. He'd been spiritual figurehead and muse, steering a disparate and somewhat dysfunctional group of men along a stumbling path he laid out for them as bohemians, outsiders, and free spirits poised between the establishment and the counterculture. Quirky songs, happenings, and left-field thinking were part of this construct for The Soft Machine. For *this* band to survive, it needed Allen's guitar clatter more than it knew.

Without him, the melodic centre shifted to Ratledge. The band had no choice. He was the only player left who was capable of taking solos. Ratledge was in the other team to Allen: team establishment, team normal, team straight. Ayers was now burdened with the full responsibility of upholding Allen's floating anarchy, but Ayers had no authority in the role. His was a career of ducking and hiding. Swiftly, and by necessity, Ratledge became the dominant voice and player, and the band became his vehicle.

And so was the dissolution sown. The more Ratledge steered the band toward a trained player's dexterity, the more he left the others behind. Ayers first, and Wyatt afterwards would be dropped in favour of more-adept and less-disruptive members. As we'll see, Ayers managed one ineffectual wrench at the controls before abandoning the band in September 1968. He could tell that Summers was a team-Ratledge player – competent, traditional – and that Ayers himself, and by extension the band's lowbrow radicalism, risked becoming marginalised. And indeed, once Ayers was out, the band brought in Hugh Hopper, now a proficient bassist with very little interest in avant-garde pop. This put Wyatt next in the crosshairs.

Hopper re-enters our story here as a member in waiting, little more than a year after rejecting Allen's offer to join. Having left The Wilde Flowers,

Hopper found himself a menial job back on civvy street, and now jumped at the invitation to act as the group's roadie. This fact would later be the cause of derisive comments, not least from later Soft Machine member Karl Jenkins. Hopper 'had been a roadie with the band, would you believe' he snorks in his autobiography *Still With The Music*. There was certainly no love lost between the pair, but the criticism is unfounded. Hopper was simply part of a tradition of players taking road jobs to maintain a foot in the business while they worked out their future – an apprenticeship in the one place the apprenticeship mattered, a bit like producers starting out as tape operators or journalists learning the ropes in the mail room. It's no reflection on Hopper's ability. It also put him near the band's steerage much earlier than we think, including his ability to woodshed ideas with his friend Ratledge while on tour together.

The band still largely played songs in autumn 1967, but this would shift as Ratledge began to compose material better suited to his leadership. Even this early, there was nothing unusual about a three-piece rock band, with or without a separate non-playing vocalist: consider The Who, Cream, and label-mates The Jimi Hendrix Experience. These power trios were the heaviest of their time.

Replacing a guitarist with an organist was less common, but even in this short period before Keith Emerson made the Hammond organ a performance piece, there was no musical reason why a British pop band couldn't revolve around its keyboardist. Alan Price, Stevie Winwood, Manfred Mann, and many others had shown that. The instrument is capable of fast runs of notes and long drones with perfect sustain, and can handle a much greater variety and complexity of chords than a guitar. By 1967, organs equipped players with a range of voices. The emerging synthesizer would extend these flavours. A competent keyboardist could play counterpoint against themselves and could even play two keyboards at once *and* provide their own bass line on pedals. The one thing the keyboard couldn't do was make as immediate and extreme an emotional connection as an electric guitar – neither the incentivising rage at one end of the spectrum nor the tearjerking sorrow at the other. And the more prominent the keyboardist's role, the more the group might stray into classicism, a template Procol Harum had laid down with their first release 'A Whiter Shade Of Pale' in May that year. Progressive rock was built on its keyboards. It couldn't have happened any other way.

Ratledge now needed to fill the room. To do so, he upgraded to a Lowrey Holiday Deluxe organ – the band's signature sound for years to come. He further beefed up his presence by feeding it through a fuzz box to a stack of Marshall speakers, resulting in a devastating blast of raw electronic power: shuddering guttural bass notes and high head-splitting shrills. Should he pause between notes, the system would shriek with feedback, so he developed a style of running the notes together into continuous warbling melody lines. With both Ayers and Wyatt thrashing along beside him, The

Soft Machine became an unremitting harangue of noise that took no prisoners and allowed no compromise. The result was a sudden leap in popularity, so much so that by the year's end, Chandler and Jeffrey had enough confidence in the group to offer them the lucrative support slot on Jimi Hendrix's tour of the US starting in February 1968.

Our understanding of all this begins with a 51-minute tape of a performance at Middle Earth Club in London's Covent Garden on 16 September 1967, released on *Middle Earth Masters* (2006). Parts of it are also scattered across *Turns On Volume 1* and *Volume 2* in inferior quality. The club was mooted as the successor to the then-defunct UFO but lasted only a few months before it, too, was bludgeoned out of existence along with what was left of the underground. At this point, Ayers was saddled with rhythm guitar to define the shape of the songs, though he switched to bass for the jazzier pieces.

As heard on *Middle Earth Masters*, the recording is of low quality, incomplete, but revelatory. It begins incongruously with the first recorded performance of Ayers's proto-calypso pop confection, 'Clarence In Wonderland', the template for his solo career. Ratledge contributes only disconnected slops of organ and perfunctory chords in the chorus. Another Ayers song 'We Know What You Mean' and a piece titled (surely retrospectively) 'Bossa Nova Express' feel just as anachronistic, though the latter does grant Ratledge the chance to lay out the melody on wheezing, no-fuzz Lowrey. *Turns On Volume 1* claims it as an early reading of 'May I'.

The set perks up, however, for a fully formed 'Hope For Happiness' lasting more than 13 minutes, beginning with the same alarming organ abuse that was later to form such a powerful feature of performances of 'Facelift'. There's gleeful malice in the way Ratledge attacks the keys for a barely constrained solo that sees him flailing over the rhythm, indiscriminately lashing out notes like curses. It's as if suddenly the band has stood upright, and everything that preceded this moment is juvenilia. There's no 'Joy Of A Toy' section yet, just a quickening of the blood into a series of brutalist extemporisations and chord stabs before we're flung back into Wyatt's vocal.

As its (again, likely retrospective) title suggests, 'Disorganisation' appends six more minutes of 'Facelift'-anticipating keyboard terror in which Ratledge delights in every bone-saw squeal, bowel-flapping bass note and wrench into feedback. It's a remarkable real time experiment in discovering just what the setup could do in the hands of a young man with near-unlimited electric power.

The set ends with punishing renditions of 'Why Are We Sleeping?' and 'I Should've Known' that seem to feature a completely different band to the one that first took the stage. This one is confident, bravura, and unfettered in its creative leaps. There's a credible debut album here in these last 40 minutes from 'Hope For Happiness' onwards, and – dare I say it – a better one than was eventually released.

Turns On Volume 1 adds an extra 11 minutes to this in the form of two Ayers songs that *Middle Earth Masters* omitted for their near inaudible vocals – a stomping 'Save Yourself' and a rough-hewn 'Strangest Scene' (later to be renamed 'Lullabye Letter') notable for some nicely in-your-face organ histrionics.

Six days later, the band were in Bussum, Holland, taping energetic versions of 'We Know What You Mean' and 'I Should've Known' for the third and final broadcast episode of the controversial VPRO television show *Hoepla*. The audio is available on *Turns On Volume 1* and a little of the footage can be seen on YouTube. Wyatt is topless, Ayers has his staring-eyed mascara and a natty hat, and Ratledge sports frilly sleeves.

Colour footage from the French TV program *Bouton Rouge* that November is also on YouTube, including shots of Ratledge with Syd Barrett-style back-combed hair and Wyatt wearing clothes. You may also find footage from *Dim Dam Dom, Ce Soir On Danse, Camera III*, ORTF radio, and others. Of the scraps of audio from the period that have been released officially, there are undated excerpts of 'A Certain Kind' and an a cappella 'We Did It Again' on *Middle Earth Masters*, and a piece retrospectively called 'Orientasian' dated only '1967/1968' on *Canterburied Sounds Volume 1*. A home tape consisting of Wyatt on guitar and Brian Hopper on saxophone, it surely doesn't fit here, regardless of its date.

On 5 December, the band performed the first of their BBC sessions, recording the five tracks best heard on *BBC Radio 1967–1971* (2003). Here are competent versions of their catalogue of quirky pop – 'Clarence In Wonderland' with mischievous bad-trip interjections from Ratledge, 'We Know What You Mean', 'Strangest Scene' with some fine key trauma, 'A Certain Kind' complete with classical motifs, and a disappointingly brief 'Hope For Happiness'.

The last official document of what had somehow become a triumphal year is half an hour of poor audio from Amsterdam's venerable Concertgebouw five days later. It's on *Turns On Volume 2*, and is presented all in one block at least. Through the murk, we hear chord changes that – with enough imagination – might be 'That's How Much I Need You Now', 'A Certain Kind', 'Save Yourself', and 'Strangest Scene'. The highlight is a squalling 13 minutes of 'I Should've Known', a wall of metal thrash above, which poke up the most punishing of Ratledge's notes. Toward the end, the piece degenerates into sirens and a shimmery rush, feasibly a drum solo.

The Soft Machine should have capped their success with an album at the beginning of the new year. They were ready, and the material was ready. But instead, they headed out to conquer America with Jimi Hendrix, taking Hopper along to drive their gear and Mark Boyle to operate the lights. Musically, the tour appears to have gone down well, though we have no official record of how they sounded on those big American stages or how accommodating the audiences were to the latest noise from the little isle.

(There's some background bleed heard in a dressing room interview with Jimi Hendrix, but that's about it.) Personally, it was every bit the rude awakening as all those movies about virgin soldiers tossed into the hell of battle. They coped through drink, drugs, and groupies.

By mid-April, it was a broken shell of a band that finally limped glassy-eyed into New York to immortalise its set on vinyl. The album only happened at all because Chandler and Jeffrey had block-booked the newly open Record Plant so Hendrix could record his third album (which became *Electric Ladyland*) and there was a four-day gap before the Experience were ready to move in.

With no time to do much of anything except roar through the live set with a few hurried overdubs, and also hampered by them being an inexperienced band in an untested studio, *The Soft Machine* has a bony, unfinished quality. It might have benefited from a more-sympathetic guiding hand and richer production, but there was no way Chandler was going to let the band overrun and interfere with his star. Instead, the sessions set up a working style that was to persist – with few exceptions – to the present day: rehearse extensively, hit the studio running, and record live as quickly as possible.

Afterwards – exhausted, demoralised, and sick of the whole business – Ayers headed off to the Balearics to recuperate. Ratledge and Wyatt found themselves back in London with the dilemma of moving the band forward in Britain. Help arrived in the form of lead guitarist Andy Summers, late of Zoot Money's psychedelic diversion Dantalian's Chariot. Here, finally, was the replacement for Allen. The pair rehearsed with Summers while waiting for Ayers to resurface, Ratledge pumping bass lines on his organ.

When Ayers did arrive, it's uncertain whether the quartet played any gigs on home soil besides perhaps a solitary Middle Earth event at the Roundhouse in May. Nine minutes of music, which purport to be from this concert were released as filler on *Middle Earth Masters*. Apparently, for legal reasons, no Summers guitar could be included on the CD, so it chose only two tracks on which he doesn't appear, 'That's How Much I Need You Now' and 'I Should've Known'. Moreover, the CD makes no mention of him. My suspicion is that if the venue is correct (and it might not be), the tape is from the Bird Ballet run of shows the band performed there in October 1967. It's not a definitive reason, but Wyatt is still singing his original words on 'I Should've Known', and May 1968 would put the gig *after* they'd been revised for the first album.

However posterity has remembered this time – Pete Frame's family tree, for example, linked Summers to the others only with a dotted line – Summers was surely brought on board as a fourth member. He wasn't filling in, acting as a session player, or augmenting a live sound: he was part of the band. It's likely he would have been an asset that steered the band to interesting places, but we have no audio record of how he sounded with them.

The reasons for Ayers's antipathy toward Summers are likely complex. For a start, it was Wyatt who suggested he was brought on board without Ayers's consent, and the band rehearsed with Summers in Ayers's absence. Ayers likely believed the band was his since he was its pinup. He was also aware of how Summers changed the group dynamic towards a more virtuoso jazz sound that excluded him. Summers's presence meant that the jolly Ayers songs would dwindle away.

As it was, Summers could have survived. The band members always hated each other, as do band members in many long-running, successful groups. That was no reason to ditch him. But the guitarist was dropped into the worst possible crucible when Chandler and Jeffrey booked The Soft Machine on a second US tour with Hendrix from July to September, and this plunge back into nightmare strained everyone's nerves to breaking point. Given Ayers's account of the tour – that he gave up drink, drugs, and groupies and vegetated throughout – it seems likely he didn't want to be there from the start and simply went through the motions. But he roused himself enough for one dramatic gesture: the ultimatum that Summers be flung out of the band or Ayers would quit. The others acquiesced. At the end of the tour, Ayers quit anyway.

It's from the tail of this tour that we begin to see Soft Machine bootlegs proliferate. We even have an official record of it – a 37-minute tape of a post-Summers gig in Davenport, Iowa on 11 August, released on *Turns On Volume 2* (or *Tanglewood Tails* if you can't find that). Through the murk of age, we glimpse a set played as a series of vicious assaults – 'Lullabye Letter', a semi-improvised variant of its bridge passage 'Priscilla', a very brief once-around-the-houses 'We Did It Again', 'Why Are We Sleeping?' divested of its elegance, 'Joy Of A Toy' transfigured to a sloppy pastiche, 'Hope For Happiness' with all the attitude of a corpse-kicking mugger, Wyatt attempting to sing 'Clarence In Wonderland' while Ayers makes disgusted droning noises, and 'You Don't Remember'. The tape ends with a tantalizing peek into the future: an improvisation that resolves briefly into the cyclical riff later immortalised as 'Esther's Nose Job'.

Subsequently, Ayers launched a perplexing solo career arranged as a series of tensions and paradoxes. Here was a man who loved the band and hated the business, but he left the band and re-entered the business. He wanted to concentrate on winsome, summery songs but the best of his solo work flies off into an avant-garde space even more rarefied than Soft Machine's. He was upset at the arrival of Summers, a competent guitarist, but he surrounded himself with some of the best guitar stylists of his time, including Mike Oldfield, Steve Hillage, and Ollie Halsall. He even brought Summers into his touring band, hatchet seemingly buried. He was desperate for at least some of the trappings of fame, and wrote singles in the sure-fire-hit styles of the day, but he ran at the first sign of success.

There was eccentricity in his work, and random, and deviance, a delight in outsiders from Syd Barrett to Nico, and in the arty set from David Bedford to John Cale, and the most pleasing of edges. He wasn't short on talent. But there's a strong case for suggesting that the strongest of his albums were sabotaged to prevent a wide audience, and that the more Ayers disfigured them the better they became. For example, when the Harvest label demanded he tour to support his first album *Joy Of A Toy* (1969), he pulled in classical composer Bedford, teenage folkie Oldfield, and street saxophonist Lol Coxhill, and with a drink-tottery Wyatt occasionally on the drum stool formed the most ridiculous excuse for a pop group he could think of. He called them (perhaps sarcastically) The Whole World, and set out in 1970 to dismay audiences with performances even more schizophrenic than the Softs', veering from throwaway ditties about hats to long stretches of free improvisation. Today the venture may be better remembered as the break Oldfield needed to write the first side of *Tubular Bells*, but it resulted in easily the best of Ayers's albums and the one work of his that Soft Machine fans will definitely want in their collections, *Shooting At The Moon*.

The Soft Machine (1968)

Personnel:
Kevin Ayers: bass, piano, vocals
Eleanor Barooshian: vocals
Hugh Hopper: bass
Mike Ratledge: keyboards
Robert Wyatt: drums, vocals
Recorded April 1968, The Record Plant, New York, USA
Producers: Chas Chandler, Tom Wilson
Label: Probe
Release date: US: December 1968
Running time: 41:23 (A: 22:05, B: 19:18)

Probe initially issued the LP in the US and Canada in an elaborate sleeve, and in Japan in a variant featuring the naked windup girl. Licensed versions appeared with inferior covers in France and Holland. It was first released in the UK in 1973 as the double set *The Soft Machine Collection* packaged with *Volume Two*. The windup girl had her bikini on this issue. There was no standalone UK release until 1976, when it crept out on ABC as *We Did It Again* with another terrible cover.

A promo single was released in the US in November 1968, coupling edits of 'Joy Of A Toy' and 'Why Are We Sleeping?' Since 2009, some CD versions include the 'Love Makes Sweet Music' single as bonus tracks. The CD version to get is the 2013 Polydor Japanese mini-LP issue, which diligently reproduces (for the second time there) the original Probe LP with rotatable wheel and all.

'Hope For Happiness' (Brian Hopper, Ayers, Ratledge)
It's probably an artifact of the album's gestation that its bookends 'Hope For Happiness' and 'Why Are We Sleeping?' both have lyrics on weighty philosophical subjects – an affectation ditched elsewhere in the band's slender songwriting canon in favour of vocal sound-play and Wyatt's musings on the here and now. This song was originally intended as raga-style hippie exotica, complete with words that wouldn't have sounded out of place in a George Harrison sermon or even from Lennon in his brief foray into open-hearted spiritualism. But within The Soft Machine's frantic onslaught, the message is entirely muted. There's a lesson here about the transience of time and the whirling gyres of fate, but you're not expected to heed it. From the opening seconds, the lines themselves are treated to the Burroughsian cut-up technique so that they simultaneously become profoundly meaningful and utterly trite.

Instead of its lyric, this eight-minute, three-part suite is all about the crazed sound world of a band reeling on the brink of dissolution, exhausted from travel, washed up in a hostile city in a strange land and skittery with first-session nerves. Regardless of the rushed circumstances of the album's creation, care was at least taken *here*. Wyatt overdubs a second layer of vocals largely in opposition to the first, his drums are treated to a harsh, head-hollowing tape delay, and there's a subtle, multifaceted presence to the production that makes it one of the band's most effective works of psychedelic pop. But it's the drive that impresses, in particular, Ratledge's post-chorus organ blast chopping fiercely over Ayers's rutted-road bass line and Wyatt's dizzy circles of fills. If there's no actual happiness in its execution – and I'm not convinced there's even the hope of some – there's certainly a sense of release, the ecstatic billowing away of a couple of years of tension.

'Joy Of A Toy' (Ayers, Ratledge)

After the first section of the suite blows itself to shrapnel, this contrasting middle decreases the tempo – if not the ferocity – for a lovely liquid riff overdubbed by Ayers on wah-wah bass on a walking bass line and more of Wyatt's tape-delay rimshots. There's no overt link to jazz saxophonist Ornette Coleman's piece of the same title, but Ayers's summery bass lines do evoke – for the only time on the album – the gloopy bliss of the Mediterranean, and hence it does form a sonic link forward to *Joy Of A Toy*, Ayers's first solo album.

But the feeling doesn't last. Having charmed us with his melody, Ayers allows the mood to thicken precipitously, slamming the listener out of their contemplation as if in rejection of even a brief diversion into beauty.

'Hope For Happiness (Reprise)' (Brian Hopper, Ayers, Ratledge)

The culmination of the suite is a triumphant recap of the 'Hope For Happiness' chorus, a restatement of its first verse rendered even more chaotic by Wyatt's cut-ups, one more blast through the refrain, and a lengthy coda dominated by Ratledge's apocalyptic organ.

'Why Am I So Short?' (Hugh Hopper, Ayers, Ratledge)

On paper, the second suite runs 13 minutes to the end of side one, and also has three sections. However, I think there are logically four sections here as, like 'Hope For Happiness' there's a repeat of 'Why Am I So Short?' after a swerve into a contrasting instrumental. The song is a rewrite of 'I Should've Known' (likely by Wyatt, though he doesn't get a credit) that crashes us unbidden into the drummer's head, a form of uncomfortable telepathy in which we learn not just physically how it feels to be Robert Wyatt, but also emotionally, and he's a mess. This confession – an aural exposure to match Wyatt's propensity to bare his skin while playing – is set to bedlam jazz rock that jerks about on a hot skillet of Ratledge's chord stabs.

'So Boot If At All' (Ayers, Ratledge, Wyatt)

Immediately after Wyatt stops singing, the suite ratchets up further for the second of Ratledge's squealing solos, scrabbling for ear space against a frenetic non-stop rhythm section and a second layer of droning organ. He runs out of things to say before the first minute is over, but the group interplay keeps the piece motoring through a brief unison riff and an outraged central stretch of belching bass, messy organ splatters, drum histrionics, and piano fake book abuse with hardly a pause in velocity for seven enthralling minutes. Wyatt finally calms down into disconnected fills and a terrific mind-mashing spill of backwards-effect skids and skitters that out-psychedelicise even 'Hope For Happiness'.

The unlisted 'Why Am I So Short? (Reprise)' returns to the self-deprecating opening stanza, lasting 17 seconds before what sounds like a tape splice shifts us straight into the suite's final section.

'A Certain Kind' (Hugh Hopper)
To balance the mayhem of the rest of the side, this is a welcome swerve into stately soul crooning. There's no charging about or kicking over dustbins but Wyatt again – there's no distinctive contribution on vocal from Ayers in the entire side – giving a faithful version of this old Wilde Flowers piece. Its power comes not from Wyatt's superb voice but from Ratledge's self-consciously church-like organ chords and blade-bright interjections. However, for all its heritage, the song feels underdeveloped, as if missing the overdubbing that might have lifted it skyward. The isolated organ riff is weedy, sucking all the energy out of the suite, and not even massed choir-like vocals and a triumphal ending can prevent it from concluding the side on an ebb.

'Save Yourself' (Wyatt)
The entire second side segues, live-performance style, forming the most substantial of the album's three suites, and one that – unlike the others – is given the scope to zigzag into surprising places. It, therefore, sets up the concept of the second album *Volume Two*, the purpose of which is also to take the listener on a sonic trip through unexpected textures and diversions.

But its start is not promising. This short opener is old-fashioned strident pop that hasn't actually progressed much since the 1967 Gomelsky demo. The vocals are awful. Wyatt hectors the woman he's addressing, and there are dreadful harmony responses in lieu of a chorus. Ratledge's vicious organ flourishes are far better, abetted by Ayers's shadowing bass as if to signal that the whole thing is merely a foul joke.

'Priscilla' (Ratledge, Ayers, Wyatt)
This spry bridge passage, lasting little over a minute, is smooth hopping jazz and a feature for one of Ratledge's more subtle organ pieces. It culminates in a disgusted bass belch by Ayers that was surely not intended as commentary.

'Lullabye Letter' (Ayers)

The title's curious spelling suggests a double meaning – that the letter is both an expression of love and a Dear John – but may simply be a mistake given that the lyric has no aspect of the latter. Another holdover from the Gomelsky demos, this is at least better-developed, with more space to unwind its meandering motifs. But there's tension between the sweet sentiment of the words and Wyatt's uncommonly gruff delivery, perhaps merely the sign of a voice roughened by touring.

In microcosm, 'Lullabye Letter' demonstrates a second, greater tension in the band. The song is not memorable, but Ratledge's solo brightens the piece significantly, his breakneck lines abetted by Ayers's fine unison work. Whatever the song itself provides, it's the instrumental that works best, and it would quite rightly be the instrumentals that prevailed.

'We Did It Again' (Ayers)

'Lullabye Letter' ends with clattering drums, a long organ suspension, and squeals of makeshift feedback, then drops humorously into the cartoon steam-train riff of 'We Did It Again' (sung as 'I did it again' throughout), which manages only a couple of circuits in its 3:49 running time. For the first time, Ayers is the dominant voice. On the second relax, a long drone teases us toward one more trip before shifting instead into the bass pedal pattern of what seems to be 'Why Are We Sleeping?' but isn't quite yet.

'Plus Belle Qu'une Poubelle' (Ayers)

Instead the suite accumulates a new round of energy for this stormy one-minute instrumental of ugly organ drones and retching bass swoops. The title translates, somewhat irreverently, as 'more beautiful than a dustbin'.

'Why Are We Sleeping?' (Ayers, Ratledge, Wyatt)

Ayers's startling, sonorous baritone is finally foregrounded in this symmetrical side-closing soul piece. It's so contrary to Wyatt's reedy neediness throughout the rest of the disc that it feels as if God himself has stepped out to address us – which, given that the song is a guileless sermon on Russian philosopher Gurdjieff, is probably the intention. But the shift from the silliness of 'We Did It Again' to this still, dark place is psychologically jolting, particularly since Ayers's muttering deity veers gradually to the wrong side of insane.

The idea of steering unsuspecting drug-dilated listeners into church is a lesson Daevid Allen took to heart when developing Gong's layering of comedy and religion, which makes it appropriate that he's evoked twice in the final verse – once by name ('Daevid is cursing') and once by reference to the nightclub of the head in which Allen had set performance poetry pieces such as 'The Switch Doctor'.

The chorus benefits from backing vocals by Eleanor Barooshian of New York band The Cake – it's a pity she wasn't employed anywhere else on the disc. She gets no credit on the sleeve, but Ayers nodded to her on the song 'Eleanor's Cake (Which Ate Her)' on *Joy Of A Toy*. While Barooshian soon faded into the crowd in Ginger Baker's Air Force, it was Ayers himself who developed the idea of prog rock anthems with soulful female backing vocals – an idea that by 1973 had transformed even the starchy old Pink Floyd.

'Box 25/4 Lid' (Ratledge, Hugh Hopper)

After the previous track dissipates on its final power chord, Wyatt's cymbal taps set up this 47-second coda, though he doesn't himself play on the piece. Instead, it's a knotty feature for Ratledge's piano and Hugh Hopper's fuzz bass, playing the 25/4 pattern of the title carefully in unison and in tight, spinning circles, each one cunningly designed to have you thinking it's the last. Indeed, the abrupt slicing-off of the final note suggests they may have kept going longer.

The First Resurrection

And so it was over. The Soft Machine had lasted just over two years – not a bad innings for a time when bands flared and were extinguished as briefly as Dantalian's Chariot were, leaving a mere single behind if they were lucky. The underground was as hostile as the beat and mod scenes before it. Longevity was not expected and almost no groups achieved it. Most of those that shared stages with The Soft Machine in 1967 were gone before them or within months of their dissolution: Tomorrow, The Crazy World of Arthur Brown, The Creation, John's Children, and many more only the cognoscenti would remember. Success was no guarantee. Cream's career occupied almost the same time span as The Soft Machine's. The Jimi Hendrix Experience lasted only a little longer, though its money wheels kept rolling for another year. Those that *did* survive adapted to yet another shift in fashion, and most carved out a whole new audience for themselves beginning in progressive rock's breakthrough year, 1969.

Nobody cared much about the death of The Soft Machine – certainly not its own inner circle. Hugh Hopper had been the first to quit, disgusted that the burden on him on the second US tour was no less than on the first. Ayers was now out and for good. Ratledge returned to London to lick his wounds.

Only Wyatt still seemed energised by the thought of continuing a music career. He'd been blessed with an iron constitution, and the two US tours had been a blast for him: endless drinking, partying, and networking with other musicians. So when the second tour was over he lingered in Los Angeles to hang out with the Experience and Summers, who'd joined his old partner Zoot Money in Eric Burdon and the Animals. In October, that band recorded *Love Is*, its equivalent of urban sprawl, on which Wyatt sang background vocals. The same month, he did the same for Eire Apparent, the third Chandler/Jeffrey signing on the tour, on their sole album *Sunrise*.

Wyatt also found studio time of his own, recording demos by overdubbing all the instruments himself, save an interjection by Hendrix on bass. Four pieces from the sessions were released in 2018 as *'68*. It's telling that everything is old. 'Slow Walkin' Talk' is a Brian Hopper song first played by The Wilde Flowers. 'Chelsa' is a Daevid Allen love song wrongly attributed to Ayers. (An Allen version from around the same time is on Gong's 1995 CD *Camembert Eclectique*.) In the perhaps anachronistically titled 'Moon In June', Wyatt amalgamates parts of 'That's How Much I Need You Now' and 'You Don't Remember'. The fourth track, 'Rivmic Melodies', strings together fragments of other Wilde Flowers songs by Hugh Hopper.

In November, Wyatt shifted to New York, where he seems to have continued working on these tracks, given that 'Moon In June' includes words about his reactions to living in the city. They're a fascinating aural snapshot of an uncertain time. It was surely too soon for him to consider a solo career, and besides, he was a band player and wouldn't contemplate stepping out on his own until his 1973 accident made live work impossible. Did he still think he was building a portfolio for The Soft Machine – one where he might play a more central role?

The songs are also musically fascinating, given that they were all eventually reworked for release. 'Chelsa' – an aching ballad of distance and longing with some surprisingly strong imagery – is a clear forerunner of 'Signed Curtain' from the first Matching Mole album. Hendrix provided the bass on 'Slow Walkin' Talk' – the beefy sound is the song's one distinguishing feature – which was first released on a Hendrix retrospective, *Calling Long Distance* (1992) and Wyatt seems to have later reinvented it for his 1975 solo album *Ruth Is Stranger Than Richard.*

'Rivmic Melodies' is album-side length and just a little judicial rework away from the Soft Machine version on *Volume Two*. Of the differences, the track is notable here for an extended, almost freeform 'Dada Was Here' with tape manipulation and a lengthy Goons-like section in which Wyatt works his way through the entire British alphabet, a bar or more per letter. This tedious exercise did survive excision, more or less, by forming the basis for 'Out Of Tunes', complete with Wyatt's aside 'T with an average amount of sugar'. The rest of the lyric is all in place, including the Spanish and the thank-yous. It ends just where the final track would turn back to the introduction.

'Moon In June' is also album-side length, but the lyric still needed work. Here it's a rueful apology to Pam, Wyatt's wife and mother of his young son Sam, left behind at home while he drunkenly slopped his way across America long after the tour ended. With retrospective ears, the most startling variant is 'so before the penguin flies.' The piece as we have it on *'68* (and, before that, on the 2002 Soft Machine compilation *Backwards*) is a complicated listen as only the first half is from the demo. The band appended the second half in spring 1969 – a much more muscular sound heralded by the sudden imposition of Hugh Hopper's fuzz bass. The rest has an identical trajectory to *Third*, including Wyatt reprising the British alphabet toward the end, and lacks only Rab Spall's violin and the tape manipulations.

The recordings are a treasure for another reason, though it wouldn't become evident until much later. With the sole exceptions of the *Volume Two* track 'As Long As He Lies Perfectly Still' (credited to Ratledge and Wyatt), whose lyric must have been coined in late 1968 or early 1969, the old Hugh Hopper piece 'Dedicated To You, But You Weren't Listening' for which he wrote new words, and a small section of 'Esther's Nose Job' which essentially used a lyric as abstract mouth noises, these were the final songs ever introduced into the Soft Machine repertoire, with 'Moon In June' the last of all.

Whatever Wyatt's plans might have been for the demos, fate in the form of Probe Records intervened in December. Probe was finally releasing the debut album that month, and wanted The Soft Machine to promote it in the US and record the second LP promised in their contract – a provision about which the band had seemingly never been informed. (The album was a minor success and Soft Machine's only charting album in the country, reaching 160 on *Billboard*.)

Back in Britain, Wyatt approached Ratledge with the news. There wasn't a band, so touring was definitely out, but Ratledge reluctantly agreed to the recording. Since swift work was needed, they couldn't go through the usual auditions for a new player and simply roped in Hugh Hopper.

The trio began frantic rehearsals. I can imagine Ratledge's sucked-lemon reaction to the '68 tape, but an album was needed and had to be filled with whatever was available – a suite based around his 'Esther's Nose Job' theme on one side, and the least objectionable parts of Wyatt's 'Rivmic Melodies' on the other. It didn't matter how bad the result was, as it was merely a contractual obligation.

Canterburied Sounds Volume 2 gives us a window into the work-in-progress, a nine-minute tape of the trio demonstrating 'Esther's Nose Job' to Brian Hopper so he could devise saxophone parts. The idea for sax may have come from Wyatt, whose scat singing on the demo (and, indeed, on the final album) might have been his interpretation of what the parts could be. While living in Los Angeles, he'd caught a live performance by Chicago Transit Authority at the Whisky A Go Go and been impressed with their brass section. He was to push for Soft Machine to do the same.

Armed with these things, the four men hurried into London's Olympic Studios and recorded *Volume Two*.

Volume Two (1969)

Personnel:
Brian Hopper: saxophones
Hugh Hopper: bass, acoustic guitar, alto saxophone
Mike Ratledge: keyboards, flute
Robert Wyatt: drums, vocals
Recorded February–March 1969, Olympic Studios, London, UK
Producer: Soft Machine
Label: Probe
Release date: US: April 1969
Running time: 33:29 (A: 17:12, B: 16:17)

The US release (stylised as *Volume II* on the labels) was the earlier, and hence may claim to be definitive, so I follow its variant titles here. It labelled the two sides as 'Rivmic Melodies' and 'Esther's Nose Job', respectively. Though the former is considered the correct way to label a side-length suite of that title, the latter is incorrect. The suite should cover only 'Fire Engine Passing With Bells Clanging' onwards. Apparently, the band were persuaded to add the individual track titles only for publishing reasons. Regardless, the UK issue (also on Probe) later that year didn't use the suite names at all, listing only the 17 tracks. In the discussion that follows, I am not at all confident of my divisions, but it doesn't matter as they are all arbitrary.

Of the variant covers, the 1977 Dutch issue is of note for throwing caution to the wind and showing a girl in her underwear on the front and Kevin Ayers on the back. No bonus tracks have ever been released on CD.

'Pataphysical Introduction – Pt. I' (Wyatt)

'Rivmic Melodies' is an outlier in an early career composed entirely of them, an aberration for a band that would not find a distinctive voice until *Fourth* at the earliest. It's the group's most overt foray into psychedelia and their most satisfying mental voyage, and the only one of their largescale pieces constructed in the classical way, bookended by a repeating theme that brings the listener back to the point of departure a quarter of an hour and a subjective eternity later. Moreover, 'Rivmic Melodies' is the band's most sophisticated amalgam of vocal and instrumental, its most obvious refraction of Frank Zappa's aural storytelling, and its most complex collision of musical contrasts, rivalled only by the more propulsive 'Esther's Nose Job' on the second side.

Even without the bolted-on section titles, and considered as a single 17-minute stretch of vinyl, it would be quite unlike any equivalent side-filling structure on *Third* and beyond: the band's most enthralling hallucinogenic adventure and a cruel hint of what Soft Machine might have become had they held together on this course. That they might have done so is not an altogether ridiculous supposition given that in 1969 a plethora of bands fostered a second wave of European psychedelia much more extraordinary than the 1967 template, including Hawkwind, Man, Gong, Nektar, a host of West German and Scandinavian groups, and Pink Floyd themselves who made psychedelic suites for years to come and to great commercial success. 'Rivmic Melodies' placed Soft Machine in the top flight of this movement, but it was again an outlier, and fans like me ache that there isn't more.

And one more aberration to note: 'Rivmic Melodies' reveals a band of sly good humour, one willing to indulge their drummer in musical and lyrical jokes and to deprecate their own pomposity. This, too, would pass.

The irreverence is there from the start. In this one-minute opener, the band come across all comical swagger in their trademark 7/8, a mock-majestic fanfare over which Wyatt welcomes us to the piece, describing it as 'a choice selection of rhythmic melodies from the official orchestra of the College of 'Pataphysics'. There are punchlines a-plenty in this one line, not least the idea of this squalling noise – from the off, Hugh Hopper's plunging fuzz bass is the dominant tone – as any kind of establishment chamber orchestra. Soft Machine had indeed received the Ordre de la Grand Gidouille from the Collège de 'Pataphysique during their dizzy love affair with the French avant-garde set in 1967, and though it's probably overstating it to claim 'pataphysics as the key to unlock the album's contrariness and flippancy, there's certainly a little junk sculpture in the disc's collisions of cultural references and random swerves, and its absurdities are fitting for a group whose very name is a combination of two incompatible images.

'A Concise British Alphabet – Pt. I' (Hopper)

The prime exhibit for the 'pataphysics is this ten-second section in which a double-tracked Wyatt sings the entire alphabet from A to Z in rhythmic blocks of four, except where W hiccups out the pattern at the end. The stereo panning on Y may be intended to provoke a question, the only remnant of the letter-by-letter wordplay from the original demo.

'Hibou Anemone And Bear' (Ratledge, Wyatt)

The album's most substantial section (running just short of six minutes) features Brian Hopper's sax overdubs for the first time, and some subtle flute by Ratledge. You will likely see the name presented with a comma, though this wasn't present on the original US or UK labels. Ratledge's gnomic title ('hibou' is French for 'owl') has nothing to do with Wyatt's down-to-earth lyric unless it's intended as a self-portrait of the trio, in which case it's simple enough to match animal to player.

Hugh Hopper drives the piece, thrusting a demonic 7/8 bass riff at breakneck speed out of the tail of Wyatt's alphabet. Wyatt skitters, Ratledge pounds the piano, and Brian lets rip on wild counterpoint lines over grinding organ flourishes. Punching out of the piece's congested headspace, Ratledge's solo sounds like a template for Caravan at its peak – you can hear Caravan's

'Nine Feet Underground' crystallising – and it's a shame that the 7/8 relaxes so quickly at 2:50 for Wyatt's lyric fragment, though the piece retains that time signature throughout. Live versions accentuated the playing and dispensed with the words.

The production on Wyatt's voice has greatly improved since the first album. He sings, attractively and intimately, of what he likes to do with his time, but he's simply making cooing noises much like 'Why Am I So Short?' on the previous disc. The words are not intended to spark psychedelic revelations. Much more allusive are the heavily reverbed sax and flute blasts that follow. 'If something's not worth saying, say it,' Wyatt concludes, an apology for his means of working: lightweight asides placed on vinyl as if they were consequential.

The section ends in the disc's most extraordinary sequence, almost 90 seconds of a Wyatt drum solo played chiefly on cymbals. It gives the lie to everything he just expressed. Those delicate taps and rolls, all bathed in the reverb, speak volumes more than his lyrics do. Toward the end, Wyatt abandons the skins altogether for escalating cymbal surges, each shinier than the last, that blast hot metal shimmers through what's left of the tripper's synapses.

It's the highest peak in the band's brief catalogue of tape used by itself for aural glitter, and it's also surely Wyatt's challenge laid down for the others to compose sound events of their own on *Third*.

'A Concise British Alphabet – Pt. II' (Hopper)
Satisfyingly spliced out of this high, the band reprise the jolly alphabet rhythm, only this time Wyatt sings it from Z to A, with W again occupying two beats.

'Hulloder' (Hopper)
With hardly a pause for breath, Wyatt launches into a troublesome section lasting 54 seconds, whose racially suspect title ('Hulloder' on the US label and 'Hullo Der' on the UK) is the least of its problems. Wyatt explains that he wouldn't want to be black in America unless he was a man of some authority, but since he's a white visitor everything's hunky. His only hang-up is being broke sometimes – the kind of clumsy comment you'd think only a man stepping over the homeless on New York streets with his face turned defiantly upwards could spout.

'Dada Was Here' (Hopper)
In another substantial section (running four minutes), Wyatt addresses his young son Sam back in the UK, ruing his absence in America, but obscuring the rawness of the emotion by using schoolboy Spanish. ('Dada' here is a pet name for 'father'.) The backing jolts in angry friction, leavened by Hugh Hopper's contrasting fuzz and clean-toned bass motifs.

44

'Thank You Pierrot Lunaire' (Hopper)

A bridge section at the end of 'Dada Was Here' seems to be Wyatt commending Ratledge on his restraint as an organist, which in turn sets up a series of lyrical gratuities beginning with 46 seconds of thanks to the three members of The Jimi Hendrix Experience and manager Mike Jeffrey for the 1968 tours. It's tempting to see Wyatt's gratitude for 'his coattails' as sarcasm, but there's no actual sign of this in the delivery. The title is likely 'pataphysical misdirection, though you could make a convoluted case for it as commentary on the clown-like submission of a 1960s rock band on a gruelling tour.

'Have You Ever Bean Green?' (Hopper)

A further 34 seconds of suspension, motorbike-style fuzz growl, and free-jazz drum clatter and elbowed piano. The most notable thing about this passage is the title (mistakenly given as 'Have You Ever Bean Grean?' on the UK label), which links back to Hugh Hopper's Wilde Flowers song 'Have You Ever Been Blue?' To my knowledge, a version of this has never been released, but I wouldn't be surprised if the tune sounded much like 'Thank You Pierrot Lunaire' since you could sing the title neatly in place of 'thank you, Noel and Mitch'.

'Pataphysical Introduction – Pt. 2' (Wyatt)

We then crash brightly back to the suite's opening 7/8 rhythm and Brian Hopper's second appearance on the album, this time comping a purposefully sloppy steal from the old jazz standard 'These Foolish Things (Remind Me Of You)'. Wyatt returns to his role as Zappa ringmaster and *We're Only In It For The Money* curtain lifter, thanking Brian and Olympic Studios engineer George Chkiantz for their roles in the creation of the piece: a glimpse at the soft machinery itself. Wyatt then blows up the entire suite with a muttered 'a few fives to take away the taste of all those sevens', implying he himself might not think too much of the ramshackle construction.

'Out Of Tunes' (Ratledge, Hopper, Wyatt)

The band duly oblige with a shift into a lunatic 5/8 rhythm, during which they gradually deconstruct over two and a half space-filling minutes of virtuosity-defying chaos. Wyatt – still muttering in sarcastic layers – again works his way through the alphabet with reprises of the demo's extemporisations, and claims he prefers quiet songs to the very 'charging about' he's inflicting upon us. So the suite busts itself to silence as if the band took axes to their own instruments. Dead 'pataphysical that, I suppose.

'As Long As He Lies Perfectly Still' (Ratledge, Wyatt)

The singletons that begin side two happen to be the two best songs the band ever recorded. This gorgeous opener expertly subverts Ratledge's clanging, complex rhythm (back in seven time) into Soft Machine's warmest moment of human connection thanks to a lovely Wyatt lyric addressed to his lost colleague. Ayers is recollected as a series of affectionate mannerisms, including his indolence and macrobiotic diet, and there are direct references to 'Lullabye Letter' and 'Why Are We Sleeping?'. But it's the peek behind the band façade that drives the song – in particular Wyatt's self-awareness ('why is the trumpeter weeping?') because no Wyatt song would be complete without it.

'Dedicated To You, But You Weren't Listening' (Hopper)
Hopper's final song contribution to the group is played as a tricky chamber piece on acoustic guitar and harpsichord. The somewhat simplistic lyric is disguised by a knotty, Burroughsian cutup that renders much of it into abstract sound, but Wyatt sings as if it has meaning. There's a little to be said for the piece as psychedelic word horde, just as there is with 'Desolation Row'-era Bob Dylan, but the appeal is largely to science undergraduates who may be turned on by references to parabolas, oxygen, magnets, geophysics, and electricity even if their mental journeys are no more profound than anybody else's.

'Fire Engine Passing With Bells Clanging' (Ratledge)
The rest of the side is an 11-minute suite called 'Esther's Nose Job' divided – even more arbitrarily than 'Rivmic Melodies' – into five sections whose titles were decided at random in the studio, mainly by stealing the descriptions from sound effects LPs. Still, it's a game worth playing. For example, this opening section is two minutes of random gloops and swirls, but the title turns it into hallucinogenic program music. The engine *does* pass and its bells *do* clang, if only in your head. For more game-playing of this type, see all the early Pink Floyd instrumentals.

   Less evocative is the suite name, which you may recognise as a chapter title in Thomas Pynchon's *V*, but that's as far as the knowledge takes you. The association-hungry voyager will soon find themselves bogged down in a distinctly non-psychedelic novel. I guess Ratledge thought he had to call it *something*, and that's more than the band could be bothered doing with large parts of *Third*.

'Pig' (Ratledge)
'Fire Engine' culminates in a sequence of throat-clearing organ chords that are in the process of fading out when Wyatt's skittery drums punch in on 'Pig', setting up the suite's central motif, a staircase riff in – you guessed it – 7/8. To Ratledge's Esher-esque piano climbing, Hopper adds the most demonic fuzz of his career, the sonic equivalent of 1990s death metal bands played at half speed. (To place this in context, while the album was being recorded, future Black Sabbath guitarist Tony Iommi was crawling back to Earth from a failed stint in Jethro Tull.)

Fifty seconds in, Wyatt leaps into the suite's only lyric. We might assume Ratledge wrote this since Wyatt has no credit, but would Ratledge really have interrupted a visceral and meticulous account of Esther's rhinoplasty with a hymn to the joys of female nudity? And why is this always considered to be 'Pig' when the words surely suggest it should be part of 'Orange Skin Food'?

'Orange Skin Food' (Ratledge)
Toward the end of 'Pig', massed overdubs of Brian Hopper's tenor sax well up beneath the rhythm. There's then what sounds like an abrupt crossfade into this section. It consists of both Hopper brothers on sax, bleating in unison over manic, bubbly left-hand organ runs and a propulsive common time for a change – though it's a rhythm turned as liquid as Ratledge's wah-wah as each player seeks ways to break free of its stifling normalcy.

'A Door Opens And Closes' (Ratledge)
Another crossfade pulls in Hugh's demon fuzz again, and we're slammed back into a particularly crazed 7/8 rhythm in which the band spits fragments of riffs and Wyatt spews insane scat-vocal interludes.

'10:30 Returns To The Bedroom' (Ratledge, Hopper, Wyatt)
There's another suspension, another punchy crossfade, and Ratledge's staircase piano riff resumes for the suite's climactic four-minute section. Hugh lets fly with more of his metal growling before a brief jazz inversion and a snarling unison blast through the riff sets Wyatt off on the album's second drum feature, this time a full kit solo. All praise to Wyatt: you can count the sevens throughout. This is followed by a sequence of swift-moving contrasts, including a second brief vocal scat, one last stab at the surgery-tight ensemble note stitching, and a full minute of organ drone and meltdown.

The Hugh Hopper Trio (With And Without Brian)

Despite the reluctant nature of the reunion, live work followed almost immediately. Within days of starting recording *Volume Two*, Soft Machine were onstage at the Royal Albert Hall supporting The Jimi Hendrix Experience. The Softs slammed through the new material, it worked, and they were running again. Gigs followed fitfully in both Britain and on the continent.

Over the next eight months, the Hopper/Ratledge/Wyatt trio built their home base audience back up – the band wouldn't return to the US until 1971 – and became one of the most extraordinary acts of the year. Hopper's fuzz bass was soon fed through twin Marshall stacks the same size as Ratledge's Lowrey set up to try to compete with his volume, while all three men challenged each other in breakneck improvisations and ensemble riffs. The songs were edged out for jazz squalls at a brain-splitting intensity as if Ratledge and Hopper were determined to marginalise Wyatt's human-sized attempt at connection.

The fact that they resorted to wearing earplugs on stage – not visible, of course, under the long hair – renders the whole idea of connection mute. The audience couldn't hear each other, and the band isolated themselves from their own noise. With Ratledge robotically impassive behind his shades, and Hopper all but unresponsive on the bass, Wyatt was the only lump of feeling flesh left on stage, and, indeed, the only one still willing to promote the band in traditional terms as human beings who engaged with the press even if not with their fans.

We have little official record of it, but we can gauge the band's live power in embryo from an excellent 40-minute bootleg tape of the Paradiso, Amsterdam on 29 March that Soft Machine released (with a misleading cover) in 1995 as *Live At The Paradiso*. The tape consists of a near-complete rendition of *Volume Two*, lacking only the first and last sections of 'Rivmic Melodies' and the all-but-unplayable 'Dedicated to You', recorded up-close in bright, clear stereo as what seems to be a single unbroken block.

'Rivmic Melodies' (its only live document, as they soon dropped it) is fixated, like Wyatt's demo, around a greatly extended 'Dada Was Here' that sees Ratledge and Hopper comping the riff in unison while Wyatt thrashes over the top, laying out his stall as the third centre of attention. But 'Esther's Nose Job' is the template for the work to follow – an amalgam of simple jazz riffs and tricky rhythms strung into a ferocious program played by all with blistering intensity.

The following month, French TV program *Forum Musiques* caught ten minutes of footage of 'Esther's Nose Job' at Ronnie Scott's Jazz Club. It's on YouTube but has not been released officially. An early, five-minute reading of 'Facelift' from an audience bootleg at Le Bataclan, Paris, on 25 June was eventually released on *Anatomy Of A Facelift* (2015), the ninth volume of the Hugh Hopper tribute set of rarities *Dedicated To Hugh*. The quality is foul, but you can just about hear Hopper rushing through the familiar changes while Ratledge produces an undifferentiated barrage on the organ and Wyatt smashes himself over the head with a metal tray.

As the material grew more complex, it was clear that Ratledge could no longer handle the interweaving lines alone, even when he placed a Hohner electric piano on top of his Lowrey. So Brian Hopper was brought in for dates in the UK. To deal with the volume, he wired his saxophone with a pickup – the same setup that David Jackson of Van Der Graaf Generator used to such effect the following year.

Brian was present for one of the odder recordings of the year, a tape of the band performing live at the Institute of Contemporary Arts, London, on 24 June, which became some of the raw materials for further manipulation. The results were presented to performance artist Peter Dockley to use as accompaniment to a Roundhouse event called Spaced. Further components were grafted on from sessions in the band's rehearsal room.

A CD of the manipulation was released in 1996 under the *Spaced* title, though with substantial latter-day edits and reinventions. Nine more minutes of the ICA show – the encore, 'We Did It Again' – were appended as a bonus track on the 2012 Japanese edition of *Live At Henie Onstad Art Centre 1971*.

Spaced is a curious art object, the first of two outliers in the band's discography alongside *Rubber Riff*. It's certainly something that would never have been considered for release at the time. But it does have one significance: when it came to the next proper album (*Third*) the same process of tape manipulation of a live performance was used for the standout track 'Facelift', while a similar deconstruction of studio components formed the end of 'Moon In June'.

No credits are given on the CD, so I've listed against each title the players you can hear in alphabetical order – assuming merely that Ratledge plays organ, Hugh Hopper plays bass, and so on. Credit should also go to Bob Woolford, who was in charge of the loop assembly.

'Spaced One' (Hugh Hopper, Ratledge)
This consists of 12 brooding minutes sounding much like an extended opening to 'Facelift', consisting of a droning organ riff looped to sound like a repeated slow-motion tumble downstairs, space object zap, noodling, clean-toned bass guitar, guitar-spring gyrations, and a percussive loop deep in the mix which I hesitate to credit as a Wyatt contribution.

'Spaced Two' (Ratledge, Wyatt)
A single seven-beat bar from what sounds like the bright central section of 'Facelift' on *Third* (or vice versa: *Third* might have used part of this performance) looped and overlain with buzzy, backwards organ that slowly grows in intensity to form a threatening swarm of electronic frippery.

'Spaced Three' (Ratledge)

We are told this is from later in the same piece as 'Spaced Two', the source tape of which apparently runs for 38 minutes. At this point, the 'Facelift'-style loop has vanished, leaving only backwards organ loops spinning around in dark, mesmerizing orbits.

'Spaced Four' (Hugh Hopper, Ratledge, Wyatt)

The standout track is this full 32-minute stretch of psychedelic squall. It begins with more 'Facelift' introduction organ drones and abuse, bass noodle, and drum hiccups overlaid with a manipulated field recording of bees. After five minutes, it begins to coalesce into a mess of cut-ups, looped and at various speeds so that no actual live source is discernible. It actually sounds most like the Grateful Dead's *Anthem Of The Sun* in the way it piles up live 'Facelift' introductions.

The sudden introduction of Wyatt's vocals at 22:37 anticipates the hellscape of Peter Hammill's 'Magog' five years later. This eventually subdues back to the bee tapes and yet more 'Facelift' layering.

Imagine the paradigm shift if an excerpt of this had been used for the third side of *Third* in place of 'Moon In June' – the deepest, most punishing trip of its time, a welcome nod to Pauline Oliveros to balance the Terry Riley, a fine repost to the Actuel free-jazz roster, Can's *Tago Mago* in genesis, a much-needed way to fend off the usual contemporary barbs that Soft Machine was simply an amped-up amalgam of Coltrane and Taylor, and a good reason to sniff at Miles Davis's more-pedestrian *Bitches Brew*.

'Spaced Five' (Brian Hopper, Ratledge, Wyatt)

The last three tracks are excerpts of a single 22-minute piece. Here's Brian's amplified saxophone fed through a wah-wah and accompanied by skewed trad jazz stylings.

'Spaced Six' (Hugh Hopper, Ratledge, Wyatt)

We pick up the piece to find it transformed into live and studio excerpts, including recognisable snatches of 'We Did It Again' (perhaps from the first LP), subject to alarming Zappa-style tape abuse over which Wyatt hammers his toms.

'Spaced Seven' (Ratledge)

Four minutes of softly keening backwards organ drones, like a haunted requiem.

Spaced wasn't the year's only strange event. In May, Pink Floyd's Syd Barrett invited the band to help him with his first solo album, eventually released in January 1970 as *The Madcap Laughs*. The trio played along to Barrett's pre-recorded guitar and vocal on 'No Good Trying' and 'Love You', in the process creating the album's best sequence. The former is terrific – like a live Soft Machine indulging an inept stage invader – but the latter is a barely together jaunt on barroom piano. The band also played a brief session that summer for Ayers's first solo LP *Joy Of A Toy*. Ayers had come back to life in the spring, and even participated in a few Soft Machine gigs to promote himself with solo renditions of some of his new numbers. As far as is known, he never sat in with the group.

Additionally, a July *Melody Maker* interview with Ratledge claimed the band were working on 'several projects' of film music. None of these have surfaced. To the same paper in November, Hugh Hopper hinted that Soft Machine were interested in composing incidental music and music for commercials, way ahead of Karl Jenkins.

On 10 June, in the midst of this busy period, the quartet entered Maida Vale to record their second BBC session. You can hear it best on *BBC Radio 1967–1971*. Two tracks were played. Curiously, neither were from the as-yet-unreleased-in-the-UK *Volume Two* but were pieces destined for *Third*: 11 minutes of 'Facelift' and a slyly rewritten 13-minute version of 'Moon In June' that, in true Wyatt fashion, simply listed the contents of its writer's mind on the day in question. The latter alone was released on *Triple Echo* in 1977.

'Facelift' is revelatory, our first clear view of Brian's integration into the live sound. The theme collapses at 4:24, leading through a freeform bridge of flute and sax overdubs into what became known as 'Mousetrap' and 'Noisette', back through a subdued 'Facelift' theme, and at 8:50 into a reading of Ratledge's 'Backwards' that wants to be gorgeous thanks to its tuned percussion opening, before Hugh's monstrous bass strips all romance away. (If it's a lovely 'Backwards' you need, then head straight for Caravan's fifth album *For Girls Who Grow Plump In The Night* (1973), where it's scored for grand piano, synth, and full orchestra.) The sequence ends with a brief romp back through 'Mousetrap'.

Finally, there are glimpses on YouTube of the trio at two of the summer's festivals. An audience member caught ten minutes of the 'Mousetrap' suite at Hyde Park on 20 September but was far more interested in showing the crowd gyrating. There's also footage from the Jazz Festival in Bilzen, Belgium on 22 August for the TV program *Tienerklanken*. The band fend off the standard questions and play a version of 'Moon In June' in which Wyatt is still declaring, out of nowhere, 'I can still remember the day my baby was conceived.' Things like that, Bob, are only memorable if they're isolated events. The best moment, though, is when an in-the-zone Ratledge whips off his glasses to reveal someone who looks uncannily like Gene Clark.

The Septet And Quintet

On 8 August 1969, Soft Machine attended the Ninth National Jazz and Blues Festival in Plumpton, West Sussex. To say they *played* is an overstatement since their performance was soon abandoned due to a power outage, but an audience recording of their brief set circulates. More significantly, it was here that the band witnessed The Keith Tippett Group, a sextet consisting of a Soft Machine style keyboards/bass/drum backline and a three-man horn section: Mark Charig (cornet), Nick Evans (trombone), and Elton Dean (alto sax). It was exactly the sound Soft Machine needed to replace Brian Hopper.

They invited the players to sit in, and in October, brought them on board on a wage alongside a fourth player, Lyn Dobson (flute). All four had roots in jazz and R&B. Charig and Dean had worked with blues singer Long John Baldry. Evans had played with Graham Collier. Dobson was a session player who'd appeared on a number of significant 1969 albums, including Humble Pie's *As Safe As Yesterday Is* and *Dragon Hill* by Britain's skronkiest man, Ray Russell.

But it was a failed experiment. The septet was too unwieldy, the egos too intransigent. The amplification required to be heard over Ratledge and Hopper was an irresolvable issue, and the fact there were now four players hanging around the stage front waiting for their next cue meant Ratledge could no longer play such long improvisations. The project collapsed within three months. Charig and Evans quit at the end of the year, and Dobson was expelled the following March. Only Dean settled into Soft Machine, and would remain part of the band until 1972 and of its family to the last of his days.

Our record of the septet live is patchy, consisting mostly of a radio broadcast and film of the Actuel Music Festival in Amougies, Belgium, on 28 October. Neither have had an official release under the Soft Machine name. However, the footage was released in the movie of the event, *Music Power*, and the 'Facelift' part of the broadcast as one track of Hugh Hopper's *Anatomy Of A Facelift*. There are also some YouTube smatterings of radio and TV shows from the continent, including live work from Théâtre National, Strasbourg on *Est Panorama* and a glimpse of the band miming in Paris on *Dim Dam Dom*.

There were no official studio recordings except for a 10 November BBC session in Manchester in which the band played a single 21-minute suite consisting of the latter parts of 'Facelift' (from 'Mousetrap' to the end) fused into parts of 'Esther's Nose Job'. This was first released on *Triple Echo* but annoyingly not in order and split across two sides of the vinyl. You can hear it in full on *BBC Radio 1967–1971*.

It's a congested big band that repeatedly intrudes on the familiar meanderings, belting sudden bright arrangements out of the snarly trio. 'Backwards' is here a vehicle for Evans's soloing, and 'Pig' an arrangement for the quartet rather than a Wyatt vocal – a disastrous change happening before his very eyes. His 'Orange Skin Food' scat is his only moment on the mike.

As if to prove he still had a voice in the band – in both senses of the word – Wyatt recorded an early solo version of 'Instant Pussy' on the same day, but the BBC refused to broadcast the piece. It's likely they got no further than the title. The song itself is Wyatt's Leonard Cohen-style account of an encounter with a groupie. It's also on *BBC Radio 1967–1971*.

Later that month, the band toured France and played on the TV show *L'Invité Du Dimanche*. Audio of an 8-minute 'Facelift' and an instrumental 'Hibou Anemone and Bear' was released on *Backwards* (2002). Both are largely vehicles for Dean's soloing. A third track 'Pigling Bland' circulates but wasn't on the CD.

There's one more somewhat obscure and mysterious memento of the septet, or thereabouts. The first Kevin Ayers BBC session on 10 February 1970, long after the septet had sundered, consisted of various conglomerations of Ayers, Bedford, Coxhill, the Soft Machine trio, Dean, Dobson, and Evans. Only Charig was missing. This unwieldy Whole World performed endearingly chaotic versions of 'Stop This Train' and 'Why Are We Sleeping?', which you can hear on Ayers's *The BBC Sessions 1970–1976*.

The quintet is much better remembered. We have a whole flush of officially released live performances from the beginning of 1970.

Fairfield Hall, Croydon, on 4 January, furnished parts of 'Facelift' on *Third* and a retrospective release *Noisette* (1999). The 19-minute source tape for 'Facelift' is omitted from that album but can be found on the Hugh Hopper retrospective *Anatomy Of A Facelift*. It's fascinating to compare it to the manipulation on *Third*. The *Anatomy* version is clipped at the start, omitting the first three minutes of organ abuse on *Third*. The two then run together at slightly different speeds (*Third* is faster) and with *very* different mixes until the main theme starts at 5:53 (*Third* time), at which point they're either completely different performances or *Third* is overdubbed to an unrecognisable extent. Following the theme, they converge again, but a long extemporisation on *Anatomy* is omitted from *Third*, which moves quickly into the fast unison riff. The crossfade (at 10:18) into and quickly back out of a separate piece of a clanging rhythm on *Third* seems intended to obliterate an awkward bridge section on the *Anatomy* tape – the two versions actually run to the same timing into the collapse into drone at 11:18 (*Third* time). Those two drone sections are not the same – Dobson's flute solo is completely different on *Anatomy* – and you can hear the splice in *Third* at 12:56, moving into the louder flute solo, at which point we're back predominantly on the *Anatomy* tape. There we remain into the reiteration of the theme. *Anatomy* fades out precipitously where it's about to move into the next piece, the point where the *Third* version lurches backwards.

Noisette documents our earliest version of what would become a live centrepiece, 'Eamonn Andrews'. It seems to have developed from a curious December episode of the radio program *The Pop Scene*, in which the band was brought into the BBC Radiophonic Workshop and asked to compose something using their electronics. Ratledge named the result after a British boxing commentator turned TV personality.

Noisette also provides our first record of Dean's saxello heading off on a crazed flight over the others (on 'Eamonn Andrews'), our first Dobson flute-and-scat excursion (on 'Backwards'), the first unashamed straight-jazz blow '12/8 Theme' (which wasn't recorded in a studio until Hugh Hopper's 1973 session for his solo album *Monster Band*), and the first time Wyatt had to sit out an instrumental-only 'Moon In June'.

The *Noisette* liner notes explain that its tape reel changes have been frankensteined with excerpts from a 10 January London gig, but that recording has not surfaced separately. Parts of the *Third* 'Facelift' were recorded on 11 January at Mothers Club, Birmingham (including, let's assume, the opening theme), but that gig's tapes also remain unreleased in full.

Our next window is a 44-minute performance at Concertgebouw on 17 January, released on *Facelift (France & Holland)* in 2022. Here we hear part of 'Facelift' with up-front Dobson flute-and-scat and harmonica solos – you can practically sense the others staring at him – and the first time Wyatt has carved out space for his vocal in a drum solo, giving the rest of the band a chance to smirk. He has a foil in Dobson, who wrongly believes he can join in.

Next comes the massive two-CD set *Breda Reactor* (2004), recorded on 31 January at Het Turfschip, Breda, Holland. The highlights of a visceral recording include a frenetic 'Eamonn Andrews', 'Hibou Anemone and Bear' played at so breakneck a tempo that it's as if the others don't want to give Wyatt the chance to sing, and a 'Facelift' introduction that piles on like an avalanche destroying an orphanage. But the highlight is a wide-ranging 'Esther's Nose Job' incorporating the first inklings of what would become Ratledge's 'Out-Bloody-Rageous.

Two poor-quality excerpts from a February concert at either University College, Swansea on the 13th or the London School Of Economics the day after are included on *Live 1970* (1998): they're the only reason to pick up that disc. They're also on *Kings Of Canterbury* (2003), the only reason to pick up *that* one. Totalling 11 minutes, we hear murky excerpts from 'Facelift' and 'Moon In June' played by a unique quartet consisting of the trio and a saxophone-playing Dobson. In the former piece, he barely hangs onto the closing riff, which may be why the others play it so slow. There's almost none of him in the latter piece, which is mostly a rumpus of Ratledge – Dobson's contribution is the wild screeching at the end.

On 2 March, the band were recorded for the French TV program *Pop 2* at the Théâtre de la Musique, Paris. Colour footage and a full two hours of audio (from the broadcast patched with an audience bootleg) are on *Facelift (France & Holland)*. It's an extraordinary document. We see Ratledge playing his Lowrey and Hohner simultaneously. We also see that the frontline pair are reading their parts, and that some of the audience are dancing ecstatically to the riffs. *There's* the lowbrow/highbrow divide encapsulated in a single image. Presumably, to prevent French grannies from slipping off their stools at home, a wildly thrashing Wyatt has decked his bareness in a woolly maroon waistcoat.

By this time, both 'Out-Bloody-Rageous' and 'Slightly All The Time' were finished and in the live set. The former is the crowning moment in the footage thanks to intense solos by Dean on alto and Dobson on soprano sax – the latter a set of subdued interweaving lines much like the composed pieces on Frank Zappa's *Hot Rats*. There's also a career-best 'Facelift'. The bulk of the piece captures an uncharacteristically restrained Dobson on flute and harmonica. Later, somebody was unwise enough to place a vocal mike within Wyatt's reach, so he uses it to unload every last twinge and grumble on a tape-echo saturated 'Pig'.

Stripped of Dobson's manic, spaced-out improvisations, the remaining quartet entered IBC Studios, London, in April to record the rest of *Third*. With the Probe contract now behind them, they'd managed to gain a favourable five-album deal with CBS, which began as favourable deals often do: with a promotional push to recoup the investment. Though there was nothing on *Third* short enough or catchy enough to play on the radio, it became the band's most successful UK release, reaching 18 in the charts. A similar promotional push in the US had less effect.

While the album feels cohesive, the work of a singular, daunting purpose, the sonic homogeny and unified sound world disguise an increasing compartmentalising between four men who no longer had much to say to each other. They didn't quite handle a side each since Dean wrote nothing, but certainly, each of the old trio had their own baby to pamper. Hopper's 'Facelift' is full of his tape experiments, Wyatt's 'Moon In June' is largely a one-man reproduction of his demo, and Ratledge's 'Out-Bloody-Rageous' sees him immerse himself in the cyclical patterns first suggested by 'Esther's Nose Job'. Each track feels like a solo work, despite the others playing on them to bind them into an illusory whole.

Only 'Slightly All The Time' recalls the suites on *The Soft Machine* and *Volume Two*, but the UK cover downplayed the divisions and the US cover omitted them altogether. This was prophetic. In the decade to come, there would never be another named suite consisting of components by more than one member – all would simply be listed as tracks – and precious few collaborations of any kind.

Third (1970)

Personnel:
Elton Dean: alto saxophone
Lyn Dobson: soprano saxophone, flute
Nick Evans: trombone
Jimmy Hastings: flute, bass clarinet
Hugh Hopper: bass
Mike Ratledge: keyboards
Rab Spall: violin
Robert Wyatt: drums, bass, keyboards, vocals
Recorded April–May 1970, IBC Studios, London, UK – except 'Facelift' recorded
live at Fairfield Hall, Croydon, 4 January 1970, and Mothers Club, Birmingham,
11 January 1970
Producer: Soft Machine
Label: CBS
Release date: June 1970
Running time: 1:15:06 (A: 18:44, B: 18:10, C: 19:06, D: 19:12)

The US and UK versions were released in the same month, so I consider the
UK issue definitive. There are minor differences in design. The only wildly
variant cover is the Japanese issue, which puts the inner photo on the outside
and fills the gatefold with text.

Luckily, the entire set fits on a single CD, so it never suffered abuse on the
format. The 2007 Sony CD added a bonus disc of the Proms performance
snappily titled 'Recorded at the Promenade Concert at The Royal Albert Hall
for BBC Radio Three on 13th August 1970'.

'Facelift' (Hopper)

Hopper's masterpiece is also the band's defining track, even though it's
extremely unlikely to ever appear on a multi-artist compilation – nor, for
that matter, has it appeared on any dedicated Soft Machine compilation save
for the 1991 *As If* cassette. The track's sheer bulk and contrariness mean
you'll get an excerpt if you're lucky, though it's the ferocious contrast of the
collage as released on *Third* that gives it much of its power. It's certainly
not due to Hopper's motif as written. I reckon I could sing you a fairly good
approximation of it, though it's much like reciting pi: the notes go *on and on*
and sooner or later, you're bound to stumble. Rather, it's the way the piece
fragments and then reconfigures its live source tapes to provide a textual rush
that doesn't relent until the last synapse-pinging backwards blip.

In addition to its importance as band figurehead and calling card, 'Facelift'
crystallised a way of working that was extended throughout *Third*. In all
four pieces (the other three sides are all studio constructs) tapes were the
source materials for elaborate sonic architecture that seems designed to be
exhausting and bewildering. That the 'Facelift' sources are already befuddling

adds a layer of complication to the piece. You won't get it on the first listen. You might not get it on the tenth, or ever. But losing yourself in its labyrinthine changes is part of the appeal.

The first five minutes of the track as presented on *Third,* are all organ nightmare: humming drones, disconnected sonar oscillations and zips of space debris, the pummelling roar of Ratledge's setup in full-on fuzz overdrive. It demands to be heard as you'd hear it in the hall, at brain-splitting volume so that every note change wrenches the floorboards out from under you. Layered behind this abuse are tentative thrusts of bass, saxophone, and other organ performances, even a buried first shrill fragment of the motif. But the tension ratchets toward Wyatt's entry on drums and the weirds of another aborted motif fragment, slaps of keening sax, and the final arrival of Hopper's Zappa-influenced motif itself at 5:53, played by ill-tempered winds.

A frenetic sequence takes over from 7:01, sax bugs splattering electric shocks over a thundering rhythm and Ratledge's unruly organ intrusions. At 10:18, we're finally manhandled out of any illusion of reality when a quasi-industrial rhythm crossfades in, only to subside itself a minute later to organ drone and Lyn Dobson's shellshocked flute solo.

At 12:56, we splice into a jazzed-up version of the same sequence bedded on electric piano, during which Dobson seems even more disorientated, struggling to find a handle on the band's remorseless seven-time as if it is some crazed mechanism set loose to clatter precipitously down an endless flight of stairs. He switches instead to sax, squalling helplessly at Elton Dean, who growls helplessly back. They've both given up before we return to the motif at 17:17, played as before by all four melodicists in unison but without Wyatt's cantering drums.

There's then something of a paradox to resolve, since in live performance, 'Facelift' ends abruptly at the end of this second run through the theme, perhaps shifting straight into something else. The band invents an ending simply by cutting to the same tape played backwards for 50 seconds. Reverse this and you hear the entire motif over, which are layered a mess of other versions playing at much faster speeds.

'Slightly All The Time' (Ratledge)
The US vinyl and some of the CD versions don't list any subdivisions for this side. However, the UK vinyl presents it as two sections of 'Slightly All The Time' with 'Noisette' in the middle. (For publishing reasons alone, this is important: 'Noisette' is a Hopper composition.) The true formulation would seem to be 'Slightly All The Time' (5:43), 'Mousetrap' (2:16), 'Noisette' (4:03), 'Slightly All The Time' (First Reprise)' (0:44), 'Backwards' (3:13), 'Mousetrap (Reprise)' (1:31), and 'Slightly All The Time (Second Reprise)' (0:40). Of all the middle sections, Ratledge wrote only 'Backwards', making this the one side of the album that is a joint

composition. It's a shame that it wasn't presented last on the LP, which would have given us three solo pieces followed by a band collaboration.

It would also be nice to consider this a composition with substance rather than merely a set of chord patterns bound together by crafty segues. It's no 'Esther's Nose Job', lacking forward propulsion. The piece's slightness extends even to its title, which was merely '11/8 Theme' until CBS retitled it without the band's input. And it's surely hard to identify the piece as a *group* work since there's almost no distinctive Wyatt involvement. On 'Facelift' we at least witnessed a drummer flailing his mallets on stage. Here, he simply keeps the beat where instructed and offers a few subtle fills. He may not have been asked for more. He likely didn't offer it.

The opening 'Slightly All The Time' was the most jazz-like Soft Machine to that point, a languid bass line over which Dean dubbed a multi-saxophone melody sounding a lot like a variation on 'Facelift'. 'Mousetrap' ups the tempo for a jumpy flute solo by Jimmy Hastings, more familiar for his work with Caravan. Toward the end Dean's saxes fade over, blowing a simple counterpoint to balance the section's overly fussy rhythm.

The altogether more stately 'Noisette' is a vehicle for Dean's slinking saxello and some Ratledge runs. A splice takes us to a restatement of the 'Slightly All The Time' motif, and then straight into the oceanic drift of 'Backwards', the side's soulful core. Ratledge's organ is all swells, and the drums are all gentle accents. Dean alternately soars and subdues like a fish leaping repeatedly at the moon.

The final 'Mousetrap' roars through its theme with skill but not much in the way of urgency, though Wyatt does at least start to move around his kit. It's a pity he wasn't given a solo here. But the momentum is swept aside for a dramatic third iteration of 'Slightly All The Time', essentially replaying the climax of 'Facelift' before resolving on a choppy chord just when you're expecting the déjà vu of a backwards tape.

'Moon In June' (Wyatt)

Compositionally, what had Wyatt done for a year? His contribution to *Third* is a straight transcription of the 1968 demo, which in turn was built from old material. Even the recording process was identical: Wyatt overdubs everything himself in the first half, bringing in the band only for the second.

This means the lyric is an anachronism, a eulogy for an affair that had already ended by the time of recording. Just as 'Dada Was Here' on *Volume Two* was a retrospective lament for time spent away from his son in America, so 'Moon In June' was a twisted memorial to Wyatt's failed relationship with the boy's mother, Pam – though it's an extremely bitter parting shot as the lyric is not addressed to her but is a blow-by-blow account of an adulterous encounter with a woman in her absence. It takes us through foreplay in brutal psychological spurts, self-justification for pushing her further, and the mechanics of the act itself, heartlessly imparted to us as a stabbing sequence of directions: 'over up over up down, down over up over up'.

The second section of the song half shifts to a wistful, perhaps post-coital homesickness. Wyatt enjoys being in New York but misses the simpler life in Kent. The third section is more disconnected – memories of home become so muddled with the woman currently in his bed that the answer to his moral dilemma is yet more self-justification. Things were already broken at home, so he can't break them more. But this is mixed with an irrelevant discourse about how the very song he's singing is just background noise, maybe even for other people doing exactly what he's doing now.

It's all a confused soul-baring that obfuscates far more than it reveals. We don't actually learn who Wyatt *is* behind all these hang-ups. It's an interesting contrast with Richard Wright's 'One Night Stand' on the same subject, released as 'Summer '68' on Pink Floyd's *Atom Heart Mother*. Like Wyatt, Wright wrestles with the morality of the strange girl in his bed but tries to understand her motivations so he can grasp his own. Wyatt wants no such communion – *his* woman is just a body to be used and disposed of, while the debate is fully internal and all but incoherent.

Still, this first half of 'Moon In June' – as the sarcastic title suggests – isn't at all to do with the depth of its philosophical argument or even the penetration of its self-examination. It's all about Wyatt's casual, chatty voice, his numerous muttered asides and seemingly random improvisations (including one half-buried F-word), and its meandering journey through his musical back pages, taking in soul, jazz, pop, and the avant-garde. He moves restlessly throughout as if he's trying to cram everything he's ever learned into nine short minutes.

In fan mythology, this track has gained retrospective significance as the final vocal on a Soft Machine studio album: the end of another era. It's even considered the beginning of the break-up, the idea (refuted by Hopper) being that the others refused to play on it, so Wyatt was forced to record it all himself. If that's not true, I bet the rest isn't, either. Surely Wyatt could have sung on *Fourth* if he'd had something to record.

At the very least, the first half of 'Moon In June' is evidence of the silence that had begun to yawn between the trio, where each became hermetically sealed within his own music and vision for the band. 'Facelift' is largely – perhaps wholly – a Hopper solo construct manipulating live tapes. 'Out-Bloody-Rageous' is predominantly Ratledge slotting band and solo sections into a construct of his own. There was no reason for Wyatt to single himself out as an outsider, but it seems that 'Moon In June' was itself a victim of the unwarranted self-pity that created it. The final complication is that from Wyatt's accident onwards we always view him through a lens of compassion. 'Moon In June' feeds into an empathy that it likely doesn't deserve.

The second half is richer, more genuine, more open with its emotional currents. Just as Hopper was robbed of a writing credit on 'Slightly All The

Time', I'd wager that the trio came up with a great deal of this in 1969. There are certainly long sections that sound like Hopper or Ratledge's way of working, even if they're slumming it in common time. Notably, this is the only side of the album that lacks woodwinds – a throwback to the time when Wyatt was scatting his Chicago-inspired lines instead.

The piece flails like a body in quicksand, collapsing repeatedly up to its waist only to somehow flounder onwards. The dinosaur-like lumbering at 14:21 is especially notable for the futility of its struggle. Seconds later, the music collapses for good, replaced by an extremely long coda of mechanical tape abuse, Wyatt's 'Out Of Tunes'-style muttering, and guest Rab Spall's squealing, time-dilated violin slurs. It's the side's most enthralling part, but its effect is muted by the obdurate mass of the song to which it's appended.

'Out-Bloody-Rageous' (Ratledge)
By the narrowest of squeaks, the longest piece on the album, 'Out-Bloody-Rageous' belies its title by providing an acreage of calm to counteract the rest of the set's flapping about, and seems to be the only piece that is clearly extended beyond its reach in order to occupy the required running time. The unnamed sections that comprise it could have been a third of their length and dispatched with far greater vigour, but there was vinyl to fill.

It is Terry Riley's minimalism – straight out of *A Rainbow In Curved Air* (1969) – that seems to fade gradually in from the silence: smooth, sonorous, dreamlike waves of organ and piano riffs looped into textures and played backwards at various speeds much like the ending of 'Facelift'. The section takes more than three minutes to reach full volume, and it is then to mesmeric effect.

But at 4:55, disappointingly, a swift crossfade jolts the listener into the same Soft Machine jazz rock we've heard twice already on the album, almost as if it's a purposeful ticking-off of tropes. It's this section that was played as 'Out-Bloody-Rageous' live, forming one of the band's performance highlights to the present day, But in truth, it's nothing special, just a different configuration of the familiar. (Play the opening section backwards, and you'll hear that Ratledge is simply restating the first bass line phrase over and over.)

At 9:54, the piece flares and dies abruptly, replaced by a second iteration of the backwards organ and piano loops heard at the beginning. These fade to silence at 10:27.

The fourth section begins as a complex chamber piece for piano, sax, and Nick Evans on trombone before another shifting at 11:05 into the same piece played on wah-wah organ, bass, pattering drums, and free-jazz sax. It accumulates power gradually, but a final held chord blows this away and at 15:51, the loops return one last time, now predominantly frantic piano patterns playing forwards (though still at various speeds), occupying all the remaining runtime. There's a surprisingly swift fade-out, bringing the band's best album to a perplexing and anticlimactic end.

The Wyatt-era Quartet

The four-piece that emerged from *Third* was the band's most stable line-up to that point. They lasted all of 19 months, an eternity in Soft Machine terms. They're also one of the fondest-remembered incarnations, and left behind another trove of officially sanctioned live recordings. But it was a disintegrating stability, and the band's immense musical strengths merely mask the rot behind the scenes. There was a trio here that had bonded into a jazz-rock powerhouse, and it wasn't the one that included Wyatt. He was the group's new fool – the one the others scorned behind his back and looked upon with amused indifference should he dare to make a suggestion in rehearsal.

Wyatt loved the band. I think he loved it more than the others did. They hated him. The more insidious the blackening atmosphere – and it was a gulf that had opened almost from Hugh Hopper's arrival – the more Wyatt pulled away and the more the separation widened. As early as May 1970, when the drummer started a side gig with his own pickup group, and then the following month when he began spending most of his time with his old mate Kevin Ayers, the band no longer seemed Wyatt's prime focus. Why should it have been when all he received was contempt?

That summer, he even indulged himself in a solo album, *The End Of An Ear*, with some vicious meanings smuggled into its title. The CBS deal that ran from *Third* to *Seven* had offered each member the chance of a disc of their own. Dean and Hopper also took up the option during their tenure in the band, but only Wyatt's is seen as a rebuke. It consists of jams involving Dave Sinclair, Mark Charig, and Elton Dean among others, manipulated, looped, and overlaid with freckled chaos. The opening 'Las Vegas Tango (Part One)' is a Gil Evans composition played as a free jam with layers of Wyatt scat like the opening to 'Hope For Happiness' but then presented ludicrously speeded up so that it sounds brittle and awkward. 'To Mark Everywhere' is gonzo trance, and 'To Caravan And Brother Jim' a corny mock-Procol Harum vamp. The best section, 'To Carla, Marsha And Caroline' mates a stately piano solo to trembling disturbances like a subliminal shifting in the darkest corner of the room.

It's not a particularly happy album in either concept or execution, which is telling for a man whose warmth and connection had helped soften the Soft Machine. (Later, like Allen and Ayers, Wyatt's post-Softs work was seamed with humour as if in rejection of the band's chilly image.) All those dedications – and they're a broad sweep of friends and former colleagues – aren't so much a rerun of the acknowledgements in 'Rivmic Melodies' as a desperate urge to connect with people Wyatt had either left behind or wished to enfold himself into like an abandoned lover. His wife Pam was notably absent, perhaps because she was in the process of ditching him for Pip Pyle, but the 'Caroline' mentioned above (Release spokesperson Caroline Coon) was soon to sweep in and out of Wyatt's life as disastrously as his tenure in Soft Machine.

In retrospect, the album's tape-loop soundscapes were an odd decision, as the logical thing for a man who complained of being an 'out of work pop singer' on the cover to do would be a *Joy Of A Toy*-style collection of songs. It doesn't jibe with the simple story to which Wyatt's biographies are condensed, that of a frustrated fan of teenage pop stuck in a band veering ever further into establishment jazz. In truth, Wyatt had always been a jazz fan, and he could certainly hold his own in even the trickiest of Ratledge and Hopper compositions. It's most likely that what he wanted was what Allen and Ayers had wanted before him – control of the group. Not necessarily to own the stage, but certainly to sprinkle the improvisations with vocal features in which the spotlight was on himself.

Another simple biographical beat would be the suggestion that the others hated Wyatt's songs as far back as 'Moon In June', and so Wyatt stopped offering them his compositions. Then where are they? There was no backlog of material to flood out the moment he was set free, like George Harrison, to fill vinyl of his own. There were almost no new songs at all until *Rock Bottom* (1974). During a scat spot on 'Esther's Nose Job' in May, he declared that he stopped writing lyrics because 'I've only got about four things to say, and I said them about two years ago, so I'm doing all the other things you can do with your mouth instead.' From this we could infer a harsher truth: his well had run dry.

It's still unclear whether all this extracurricular activity in summer 1970 was intended as a permanent split. ('I'm not killing off the Softs,' he assured *Melody Maker*.) The others approached Phil Howard with the idea that he would either deputise for or replace Wyatt, but in the event, Wyatt came back as if all was forgiven, and the sound that greeted the December release of *The End Of An Ear* was mainly the others' collective sigh of relief that it was as indulgently uncommercial as *Spaced*.

The failure of *The End Of An Ear*, and the abandonment of his extracurricular work with Ayers, didn't mean Wyatt committed himself back to the parent group. He continued to be a session player on call throughout the rest of his time in the band, perhaps revisiting the period in the autumn of 1968 when he'd hung around in the US hoping to be magically spirited into a rock band. He appeared on Lol Coxhill's *Ear Of Beholder*. He gigged with jazz group The Amazing Band alongside Mal Dean and Rab Spall, including playing on their album *Roar*. He supported Keith Tippett on *Dedicated To You, But You Weren't Listening* and became a member of his big band Centipede (alongside Roy Babbington, Mark Charig, Elton Dean, Nick Evans, Karl Jenkins, John Marshall, and 43 others), including a tour and playing on the vast, unruly, and incomplete *Septober Energy* produced by Robert Fripp.

In December 1970, Wyatt began gigging with a band of his own, Symbiosis (for at least one performance billed as 'Soft Robert'), whose members included Tippett, Babbington, jazz saxophonist Gary Windo, and trumpet player Mongezi Feza. This aggregation sounds thrilling in principle, but it didn't leave behind much of an official record and struggled for six months before abandonment. You can hear its stampeding 11-minute instrumental 'Standfast' (recorded for the BBC in January 1971) on Wyatt's 1994 compilation *Flotsam Jetsam*, and 30 seconds of 'NTU' (from the same session) on Windo's *His Master's Bones* (1996). Symbiosis was one of the plethora of Soft Machine spin-offs at the 7 February Roundhouse show but didn't make it onto Allen's *Live At The Roundhouse 1971*.

Meanwhile, it was a demonstration of Elton Dean's improved status in the band that he persuaded the others to reduce their volume, enabling him to ditch the hated mouthpiece pick-up and use a microphone instead. This quieter Soft Machine became, by nature, more contemplative, more a standard fusion and free-jazz ensemble. Dean even shifted to Fender Rhodes electric piano at times, forming layers of counterpoint to Ratledge's leads.

Of course, as Dean became ever more a team man, so Wyatt became ever more of a loner. But this isn't just about how the drummer felt. The cloud of unhappiness surrounding him inevitably affected the others, who – despite their personas – were not the automatons they seemed to be. For Ratledge, *Third* was the turning point. From now on, the band became a trial for everyone, but it was money, a living, and a career, and the French adored them.

So the machine clattered on, now playing a largely heads-down set predominantly of convoluted Hopper and Ratledge jazz lines to which Wyatt obstinately added his continuous barrage of drunken Mitch Mitchell-style drum thrash, a sort of sonic territorial pissing that did nothing but aggravate the others. This put him in an untenable position. If his understanding of the band was simply to hit everything as a one-man noise maker, then he had as little grasp of the nuances and possibilities of progressive rock as he did of jazz. You couldn't imagine Bill Bruford carving out a long career with the same attitude and, in retrospect, you couldn't imagine Wyatt lasting through the 1970s as a drummer any more than Mitchell did. The alternative was equally unlikely. Wyatt wanted to be a singer, but how could he sing if he didn't want to lead a band? And why cling to Soft Machine when he and the group offered nothing meaningful to each other?

There's great music here. Maybe the greatest of the band's career. But we listen to it through gritted teeth.

Our window into the quartet opens on a run of shows they played at Ronnie Scott's jazz club during the *Third* sessions. It was a surprisingly long engagement, lasting six consecutive nights. One unidentified performance was released as *Somewhere In Soho* in 2004. The set was their then-standard one, comprised of arrangements of all four *Third* pieces plus 'Hibou Anemone and Bear' and 'Esther's Nose Job' from *Volume Two* and the unrecorded pieces 'Eamonn Andrews' and 'Pigling Bland'. The former didn't make it to an album, but the latter was eventually recorded in the studio for *Fifth*. There are no vocals except for a couple of brief scat sections.

The sound is not outstanding. But from the opening moments of 'Slightly All The Time', the new approach was already in evidence in this more intimate venue: clean bass rather than monstrous fuzz, Ratledge's nuanced electric piano playing, and crisp saxophone runs. The problem *was* Wyatt, however, we sugar-coat it to match our sympathies. His understanding of his role hasn't shifted – rush through everything, cram every second with fills, and subtlety be damned. Wyatt sabotages the performance from the start, meaning that by the end of 'Slightly All The Time' Hopper has given up and kicked the fuzz back on.

The effect is repeated to the end of the tape: pieces that blow beautifully but become ever more unbalanced whenever Wyatt asserts himself.

The day after the Ronnie Scott gigs ended, Soft Machine took the set to Fairfield Hall, Croydon. From this performance came the recording *Facelift* (2002), not to be confused with the *France & Holland* release. Sonically, it's even worse than *Somewhere In Soho*, effectively just another audience tape, even if the audience member holding the cassette deck on his lap was Brian Hopper. The distant, boxy sound makes a chore of what Hopper claims was a peak performance. But stick it out for a riveting 'Eamonn Andrews' that seems upside-down, back-to-front, and skewed to the guts – and all the better for it. There's also an improvised romp through 'Why Am I So Short?' (titled 'I Should've Known' on the CD) with Wyatt actually singing some words.

The first of a host of BBC sessions for the quartet – a return trip to Manchester on 4 May – saw a 19-minute amalgam of 'Slightly All The Time', 'Out-Bloody-Rageous', and 'Eamonn Andrews'. It was released in truncated form on *Triple Echo* but is available unedited on *BBC Radio 1967–1971*. It's mostly relatively genteel chamber music divested of the live fire, portending an even more calculated studio approach.

Chronologically, the final excerpt of the CD *Backwards* consists of 39 minutes from 'late May, 1970, in London', according to the cover. It's actually another BBC performance, this one for its *In Concert* strand recorded on 21 May at its dedicated 400-seat Paris Theatre. Let's assume there was an audience, and even John Peel doing the introductions, though there's no sign of either on the CD. Wyatt shifts 'Moon In June' into his 'Pig' rant, and this is the gig where he makes his 'I've only got about four things to say' comment.

A few minutes of the band playing 'Esther's Nose Job' at the Holland Pop Festival in Kralingen, Holland, made it into the movie *Stamping Ground*. Like Amougies the year before, the band have not released this footage themselves. It shows that here, at least, Dean is back on the bug.

Soft Machine reached their greatest visibility and the zenith of their establishment outreach on 13 August when they became the first rock group to perform at the annual Henry Wood Promenade Concerts (known as 'The Proms') at the Royal Albert Hall, London. Incidentally, this was nothing to do with the 'Pop Proms' headlined by Led Zeppelin and held in the venue the previous year, which merely co-opted the name. We can assume Soft Machine

Left: Canterbury band The Wilde Flowers included two future Soft Machine members: Hugh Hopper (left) and Robert Wyatt (in pipe). Without them, the group eventually evolved into Caravan.

Below: The Daevid Allen version of The Soft Machine lasted just over a year and released only one single. Left to right: Wyatt (drums), Allen (guitar), Kevin Ayers (bass), Mike Ratledge (organ). (*Alamy*)

Left: The band continued as a trio after Allen's departure. This is the back panel collage from their first album, normally hidden behind a die-cut wheel. Clockwise from top: Ayers, Ratledge, Wyatt. (*Probe*)

Right: After Ayers also quit, bassist Hugh Hopper was brought in. By early 1970 (as shown here), they had become a quintet. Left to right: Lyn Dobson, Elton Dean, Hopper, Wyatt, Ratledge. (*Courtesy of Cuneiform Records*)

Above: The classic quartet of (left to right) Ratledge, Hopper, Wyatt and Dean saw the band at the height of its acclaim. Here they are outside the Royal Albert Hall in August 1970. (*Alamy*)

Below: By 1975, Ratledge was the only original member. This is the quintet that recorded *Bundles*. Left to right: (rear) Karl Jenkins, Ratledge, John Marshall, (front) Alan Holdsworth, Roy Babbington. (*Tony Russell*)

Left: The band's untitled first album was released in December 1968 in an elaborate sleeve reminiscent of Manfred Mann's 1966 EP *Machines*. (*Probe*)

Right: Part of the original back cover. In later issues, Probe tried to censor the model by painting on a bikini.

Left: Probe went right ahead with another naked girl for this disturbing *Volume Two* (1969) cover, in which a robot sex doll seems to be removing its mask to reveal a real human hidden inside. (*Probe*)

Right: Despite a hermetically sealed brown-paper-effect cover, *Third* (1970) still stands as one of the most remarkable albums ever made. (*CBS*)

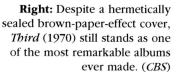

Above: Would you feed your daughter to this room? The inner spread of the UK version of *Third* shows the band in a journalist's apartment in Cologne in April 1970. Left to right: Dean, Hopper, Ratledge, Wyatt. (*Photo by Jürgen D. Ensthaler*)

Right: Wyatt's last release *Fourth* (1971) is well remembered but regarded as being as emotionally cold as Ratledge's folded arms. (*CBS*)

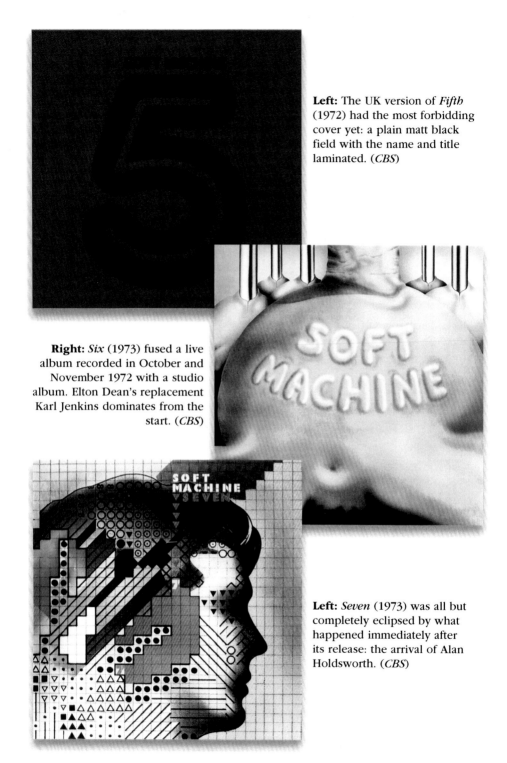

Left: The UK version of *Fifth* (1972) had the most forbidding cover yet: a plain matt black field with the name and title laminated. (*CBS*)

Right: *Six* (1973) fused a live album recorded in October and November 1972 with a studio album. Elton Dean's replacement Karl Jenkins dominates from the start. (*CBS*)

Left: *Seven* (1973) was all but completely eclipsed by what happened immediately after its release: the arrival of Alan Holdsworth. (*CBS*)

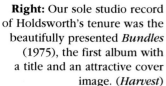

Right: Our sole studio record of Holdsworth's tenure was the beautifully presented *Bundles* (1975), the first album with a title and an attractive cover image. (*Harvest*)

Left: While recording *Softs* (1976) with Holdsworth's replacement John Etheridge, Ratledge withdrew quietly from sessions, the band and the business. Old fans might not even notice him missing from the cover. (*Harvest*)

Right: *Alive and Well Recorded in Paris* (1978) is the only document of the band's final two years. It commemorates a lineup consisting of Etheridge, Jenkins and Marshall, plus bassist Steve Cook and violinist Ric Sanders. (*Harvest*)

Above: Mike Ratledge was central to Soft Machine throughout all the turmoil of its peak years, though he later admitted he hadn't much enjoyed being in the band after *Third*. (*Gijsbert Hanekroot*)

SOFT MACHINE
RUBBER RIFF

Left: During the *Softs* sessions, Jenkins roped the others into helping out on a solo project of library music for De Wolfe. The original cover had no performer name (simply the words 'Music De Wolfe' over the title). Since 1994, it has been credited to the band, as shown here. (*Voiceprint*)

Right: *Land Of Cockayne* (1981) is essentially another Karl Jenkins solo project released under the band name. (*EMI*)

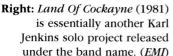

Left: *Soft Heap* saw former members Hugh Hopper and Elton Dean join with Alan Gowen of Gilgamesh and Pip Pyle of Hatfield and the North. Their only studio album was recorded in October 1978. (*Charly Records*)

Right: *Soft Works* was the first project to consist entirely of old Soft Machine members. The cover of *Abracadabra* (2003) shouts its attributes proudly. (*Tone Center*)

ELTON DEAN   HUGH HOPPER

ソフト・マウンテン

SOFT MOUNTAIN

HOPPY KAMIYAMA   YOS

Left: While on tour in Japan in August 2003, Hopper and Dean played a live-in-the-studio jam with two notable local musicians, released as *Soft Mountain* (2007). (*Hux Records*)

Right: Though the previous projects had tiptoed around the parent name, Soft Machine Legacy (consisting of Hopper, Dean, Marshall and Etheridge) made it blatant on their eponymous studio album (2006). (*MoonJune Records*)

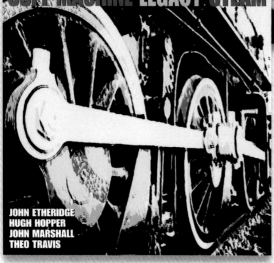

Left: Dean's ill health saw Theo Travis step in on woods for the studio album *Steam* (2007). One of modern jazz's unrecognised grand masters, Elton Dean passed away in 2006. (*MoonJune Records*)

Right: When Hopper died in 2009, Etheridge, Marshall and Travis brought in our old friend Roy Babbington. Their first studio album *Burden Of Proof* was released in 2013. (*MoonJune Records*)

Left: In 2015, the group struck the 'Legacy' from their name. *Hidden Details* (2018) was packaged in a mushroom-head design that is, let's be fair, the best cover since *Bundles*. (*MoonJune Records*)

Right: *Other Doors* continues the striking packaging of *Hidden Details* with new ways to express the disturbing *Volume Two* automaton. (*MoonJune Records*)

Left: *Middle Earth Masters* (2006) documents an Ayers-trio gig at the London club in September 1967, as well as oddments from November 1967 and May 1968. (*Cuneiform Records*)

Right: During the band's hiatus in late 1968, Wyatt recorded a number of demos in the US. An album's worth, including 'Moon In June', was released 50 years later on *'68* (2018). (*Cuneiform Records*)

Robert Wyatt
'68

Left: *Spaced* (1996) was an edited release of experimental music recorded in June 1969 for an art installation and performance by Peter Dockley. (*Cuneiform Records*)

Right: The quintet with Lyn Dobson is well documented by retrospective live releases. One of the best is *Noisette* (1999), live in Croydon in January 1970. (*Cuneiform Records*)

Left: You can hear drummer Phil Howard's full impact on the band on *Drop* (2008), recorded in West Berlin in November 1971. (*Moonjune Records*)

Right: Recorded live in Rotterdam in October 1973, *The Dutch Lesson* (2023) is an excellent reminder of an overlooked moment in the band's history. (*Cuneiform Records*)

4 Sides.
4 Songs.
Because Soft Machine Needed More Time To Play.

No song on this album is under seventeen minutes.
In England where it was first released, they compare Soft Machine to Pink Floyd and King Crimson. They speak of Mike Ratledge's organ playing in terms of Frank Zappa's guitar.

In fact in the U.S., *Fusion* said, "His work here as sort of a trail blazer for Soft Machine far and away exceeds the past efforts of any of popdom's top organists."

And in *Rock*, David Reitman said: "The Soft Machine have made here the first successful exploration of one direction rock can go...the long, improvised, instrumental direction...(they) have taken rock playing, rejuvenated it, made it interesting, saved it for the future...I am no longer afraid music will die of sterility...they are showing us the way."

No song is under seventeen minutes. Because Soft Machine wanted the time to coddle and develop their musical ideas.

No song is under seventeen minutes. Because if music is going to grow, it has to have room.

On Columbia Records

A specially priced 2-record set.

Above: Full-page adverts like this one from *Rolling Stone* helped make *Third* a success. Actually, the shortest 'song' on the album runs to more than 18 minutes.

Right: Soft Machine were still associated with Zappa-style psychedelia as late as 1972, according to this US advert.

DON'T BE ALARMED IF YOU SEE THINGS WHILE LISTENING TO THE NEW SOFT MACHINE ALBUM. THERE'S NOTHING WRONG WITH YOU.

As every good rock Anglophile already knows, Soft Machine is way ahead of their time. Their instruments paint exquisitely textured images across your auditory nerves. Imaginative. Surreal.

David Reitman wrote in *Rock*, "Their music is strange, mystical, modol, cacaphonous, but also swinging and wailing —you can never predict what will occur next."

The new Soft Machine album, 5, broadens their view still farther. Open your ears. And see.

On Columbia Records and Tapes

SOFT MACHINE 5

KC 31604

Below: This *Rolling Stone* advert features the US cover of *Seven*. Clockwise from top left: Babbington, Ratledge, Marshall, Jenkins.

You're looking at the four most acclaimed musicians in England.

Soft Machine has made a shambles of England's prestigious *Melody Maker* Reader's Poll.
Mike Ratledge:
    Organist of the Year.
John Marshall:
    Drummer of the Year.
Karl Jenkins:
    Miscellaneous Instrumentalist of the Year.
"Soft Machine Six":
    Record of the Year.

Yet over here in the colonies, they are less than a household word. But maybe now that people have picked up on Pink Floyd and John McLaughlin, they're ready for "Soft Machine Seven."
    The critics are ready. For years they've been raving when it came to the Softs.
    So, obviously, it's high time America found out what England already knows: Soft Machine is one fine band.

**"Soft Machine Seven."
On Columbia Records**

Left: *Out-Bloody-Rageous* (2005) is probably the best entry-point compilation. It includes both sides of the 1967 single 'Love Makes Sweet Music', but for licensing reasons, carries the story only up to *Seven*. (*Sony*)

The current Soft Machine line-up sees a band rejuvenated and as inventive as ever. Left to right: John Etheridge, Asaf Sirkis, Theo Travis, Fred Thelonious Baker. (*John Bentley*)

were broadcast live on radio in the homes of many more than attended the event, at least for a short time, though the season is generally ignored by the masses until the flag-waving finale.

The establishment reacted – as doubtless provoked purposefully by that night's program director, Tim Souster – with a hissy fit. But for every sneer, there was a commentator with ears, including those in jazz and classical voice pieces, who understood the band's role in narrowing the last of the rapids that divided the dwindling island of dinner-suit snoots from the mainland rabble of unwashed dope-smoking freaks.

In truth, it scarcely needed to be Soft Machine at all. It could have been Pink Floyd with their newly minted 'Atom Heart Mother' or Deep Purple with the concerto they'd performed in the Hall almost a year earlier. The timing was even right for Frank Zappa's *200 Motels* (the 1970 suite, not the 1971 soundtrack). He'd played the Hall too. Every pop group with the cash had played the Hall.

Lucky or not, Soft Machine pioneered something that today seems so commonplace it's hard to believe there was ever actually a fuss about it. But the band's retort that they never repeated the experiment because it made them uncomfortably highbrow is wishful thinking. All but Wyatt would have been delighted to stay in that space, but they didn't have the choice. Sure, they could go back to playing London's Royal Festival Hall, Liverpool's Royal Philharmonic Hall, the Concertgebouw, and other establishment venues on the continent – and sure, the French avant-garde crowd would always support them – but they were never going to attract the frocks and tuxes to their gigs. Shaggy rockers with their hair tucked inside the temples of their shades would not become the new elite, even if Dean persisted in reading his parts off manuscript – not without killing off the old elite first, and it would take rock a few more decades to do that.

Audio of the event has been released at least three times officially. The best source to grab is the 2007 two-disc version of *Third*. The strict schedule allowed only a 39-minute set of three numbers: 'Out-Bloody-Rageous', 'Facelift', and 'Esther's Nose Job'. The first piece begins delightfully with the album's tape loops used as walk-on music and the alarming static cracks of the crew trying to boot Ratledge's organ into life. It's over four minutes before the organist makes his entrance. But the performance seems stilted, as if the occasion has rendered all four players constipated. By the point they've warmed into the concert in 'Esther's Nose Job' it's all but over.

As far as I know, the band hasn't sanctioned release of the TV footage first broadcast on the BBC *Omnibus* strand ten days later. Nor do we have official versions of radio sessions in France and Spain in August, a BBC *Sounds Of The 70s* concert at Camden Theatre, London, on 17 September, or the band's purported rendition of the fresh-minted Dean piece 'Neo-Caliban Grides' on BBC TV program *Anatomy Of Pop* a month later. The composition has never been released on a Soft Machine studio album but did appear in

1971 on Dean's first solo album. Its title ('Caliban' being the beast-man in Shakespeare's *The Tempest*, and 'gride' a harsh cutting sound) would appear to be a snark at the establishment's dismissal of the band as a new type of savage making unpleasant noises.

Third was barely in the stores when the band returned to the studio in two factions for ten days in October and November to record the opportunistic follow-up *Fourth* – their first album to dispense with vocals altogether, and the first without any Wyatt compositions. But he does get a desultory peek out from the front cover. French TV filmed a ten-minute window into the sessions, which is available on YouTube but has not been released officially. We see Ratledge coaching session bassist Roy Babbington, Hopper on his new Fender Jazz bass, and Wyatt leaping about, filling the space with musical ideas that the others ignore. To be fair to them, the camera is on Wyatt and he knows it, making the session somewhat atypical. Regardless of its surliness, *Fourth* was another success, reaching 32 in the British charts.

Between the two blocks of recording, Soft Machine headed over to Amsterdam for the 25 October gig at Concertgebouw, which was beautifully recorded and released as *Grides* in 2006. Here we hear the first proper 'Neo-Caliban Grides', a back-alley knife fight between sax and keyboards escalated by Wyatt's goading snare and Hopper's psychotic bass. There are also three-quarters of the *Fourth* material: a near-complete 'Virtually' in which Wyatt seems too busy counting sevens to indulge in his usual deconstruction of the rhythm and an embryonic 'Teeth' that slaps around the stage without ever deciding which pot to boil itself in. To fit these two pieces in the set, the band reduces 'Facelift' and 'Eamonn Andrews' to perfunctory trots through their themes, and 'Esther's Nose Job' is about to disappear altogether. But the highlight is a subdued two-part 'Slightly All The Time' where four heavyweight players find intelligent ways to circle the ring without squashing each other flat. Throughout the concert, when he's not spinning out dizzy alto-sax runs, Dean skips back to his Fender Rhodes to thicken the harmonies. There's no Wyatt vocal whatsoever.

The band were back in the BBC studios twice in December, first when Ratledge and Wyatt joined in John Peel's traditional holiday japes by singing carols along with a host of other rock stars, and then on the 15th for a 20-minute Maida Vale session of 'Virtually' and 'Fletcher's Blemish' from the upcoming LP. You can find these two on *BBC Radio 1967–1971*.

Wyatt is much more confident to slither all over 'Virtually', adding a welcome complexity to the one-chord jam that forms much of the piece's first half. The focus is the mid-point abuse of Ratledge's elderly and ailing Lowrey, around which the rest of the piece clusters as if transfixed. Dean (on saxophone) and Hopper provide sympathetic echoes. 'Fletcher's Blemish' is uncomfortable free jazz with Ratledge on piano and gabbling organ, repeatedly chaperoning itself into the makings of the archetypal Soft Machine groove with snatches of snarly riffs before flying off again to stunned reconfigurations.

Compared to all this action, 1971 saw less frenetic activity and the yawning of an irresistible black hole into which Wyatt was being pulled. Our earliest window into it is the band's hour-long TV performance on *Pop Show* at Théâtre 140, Brussels, Belgium on 15 January. This hasn't been released officially, but is currently available to view on YouTube. Soft Machine have a thrilling intensity, as if they've started the year with a hunger that will soon dissipate.

The second window – *possibly* officially released – contains no actual music at all. It's manager Sean Murphy's vehement stage announcement at the Palais de Sports, Paris on 31 January, after the concert was cancelled due to audience unrest. When he's not spewing anger at the police, Murphy begs the rioters not to damage the band's equipment. You can hear it on *The Mystery And The History Of The Planet Gong*.

Next came a two-day event in Høvikodden, Norway, on 27 and 28 February. From the first night, only 'Facelift' has been released, on the Hugh Hopper retrospective *Anatomy Of A Facelift*. The entire second night set is available as the three-disc set *Live At Henie Onstad Art Centre 1971* (2009). According to the cover, the band performed 'two continuous sets of compositions, improvisations and dynamisms' that were 'processed with electronic effect devices'. It came with a CD-ROM of academic analysis titled 'The Soft Machine Sound: An Electronic Acoustic Experience Examined' – exactly as you'd expect from an art-centre project. The Proms were unacceptable, but *this* was the space Soft Machine thought they should occupy?

The contents were actually the familiar *Fourth*-era set. The entire new album was performed, along with three-quarters of *Third* (omitting 'Moon In June'), 'Eamonn Andrews', 'Neo-Caliban Grides', and two pieces that would be released on *Fifth*: 'All White' and the already-familiar 'Pigling Bland'.

Given what was expected of the band – that this was essentially a living installation – they play freer than in concerts where the audience would have expected all the usual riffs and rhythms, using each piece's themes as springboards into extemporising. Dean concentrates on electric piano, which effectively means that compositions like 'Facelift' are back to the 1969 trio format with Ratledge as the sonic core. When Dean returns to blowing, it's to add organic warmth that humanises pieces like 'Slightly All The Time' and 'Out-Bloody-Rageous' and prevents the whole thing from degenerating into gallery sterility. Wyatt, too, seems less inclined to batter and more to lean on tangled patterns of mallet and bare-hand tom fills, though he does perk up for a frenetic 'Teeth'.

On 11 March, the band returned to the Paris Theatre for another BBC *In Concert* showcase – best heard as *Soft Machine & Heavy Friends: BBC In Concert 1971* (2005) – on which a host of other musicians supported and augmented the quartet. Happily, John Peel *is* present on this release, and talks us through the planned set so we can at least visualise which faceless players are making the sounds.

First, there's a rendition of Dean's 'Blind Badger', destined for his solo album recorded two months later and played by that album's line-up of Ratledge (keyboards), Mark Charig (cornet), Phil Howard (drums – eventually to become Wyatt's replacement in Soft Machine), and Neville Whitehead (bass). Whitehead is one of a host of peripheral Softs characters. He never joined the group, but he had played bass for Wyatt's *The End Of An Ear* album.

There's little to separate this line-up from the parent group. Howard is a slightly more kick-drum-happy player, and Whitehead sticks to a clean tone, but the written lines, squally blowing, and free-jazz are identical.

Howard stays to accompany the regular quartet as second drummer on a short but understandably ferocious 'Neo-Caliban Grides'. The rest of the concert is the quartet doing an abbreviated set, accompanied on the centrepiece 'Teeth' by a sort of surrogate septet front-line of Charig, Ronnie Scott (tenor sax), Paul Nieman (trombone), and another future Softs member Roy Babbington on double bass. The core band seem as worn-out as their equipment, brought painfully to a sort of sonic pathetic fallacy by the fractious static that intrudes on 'Out-Bloody-Rageous'. The guests lift them a little, bringing back memories of that moment in late 1969 when the possibilities seemed endless, but the crazed blowing is paper on an undressed wall. You can still see all the bumps.

The band were back at Het Turfschip, Breda, Holland, on 21 March. From here, a rendition of 'Facelift' has been released on Hopper's *Anatomy Of A Facelift*. Two days later, they recorded two performances at the Gondel Filmkunsttheater in Bremen, West Germany. First was a set captured on video for *Beat-Club*. Only 20 minutes were broadcast, later appended as a DVD on the *Grides* release. The footage suffers from the standard psychedelic *Beat-Club* overlay, but we do see some very battered gear, Dean and Ratledge looking bored, Wyatt with what now seems like a ridiculously small kit, and a spider-fingered Hopper resplendent on a stool. In retrospect, Wyatt's vocal improvisation looks like a naked cry for help, though seemingly the others wouldn't have cared if he'd leaned over and slit his throat on a cymbal.

They then ran through their full stage show for Radio Bremen. This was released in 1998 as *Virtually*. Being in a studio with a small audience, the performance has the feel of the Henie Onstad Art Centre event: a group of players liberated to explore the music for themselves. Its greater engagement than the *Beat Club* performance suggests that Soft Machine were now all about a stage dynamic that had much to do with scrutiny and invasion. The band would put their collective heads down and play a continuous set with no interval, neither soliciting nor responding to the energy of the hall. The size of the audience seemed to make little difference.

Take note of Wyatt's somewhat manic vocal improvisations during 'Fletcher's Blemish' and 'Eamonn Andrews'. They were the last official public excursions we were to hear from him with the band.

Our final quartet release is a short set of three pieces recorded for the BBC at Maida Vale on 1 June, best heard on *BBC Radio 1967–1971*. There's a stormy but shapeless 'Neo-Caliban Grides' and a fine suite consisting of 'Eamonn Andrews' and 'All White'. But posterity declares the most significant piece to be a solo Wyatt rendition of 'Dedicated To You, But You Weren't Listening' on piano and echoed vocal, complete with primitive clicks as he switches the effect on and off.

In the midst of the band's terminal crisis, their prospects couldn't have been brighter. A short US trip in July saw them mixing with their heroes, including playing support to Miles Davis. A poor quality audience tape circulates from The Gas Light, New York, apparently on the first date of the tour. But things came to a head later in July, in the traditionally British manner of band break-ups. Wyatt unwisely mentioned at Ronnie Scott's that he wished he could find another band, and the others snarled back that he should go ahead and leave if that was his attitude. By some accounts, he'd actually walked out on the band many times before, only to stumble back in as if nothing had happened just like he did in the summer of 1970. This time, there would be no open door.

Wyatt's depression would take years to lift. At first, he lay low and turned even further inward. He drank. He despaired. He attempted suicide for at least the second time, slashing his wrists and thereby succeeding only in sundering his relationship with Caroline Coon. He surfaced most visibly in November 1971 at the Berlin Jazz Festival, where he sat in with Don 'Sugarcane' Harris, and joined Harris and Jean-Luc Ponty in a set billed as New Violin Summit. Wyatt even fended off workable offers, including the possibility of being John Marshall's replacement in Nucleus.

At the end of the year, he finally formed Matching Mole, a band that would marry the improvisatory ethos of Symbiosis to the pop sensibilities of early Soft Machine in lunatic collisions inspired by those of Ayers's band The Whole World. Its original line-up included Caravan's keyboard player Dave Sinclair, Delivery guitarist Phil Miller, and bassist Bill MacCormick. But whatever its intentions, Matching Mole was another unhappy amalgam from its backwards-facing name downwards. Sinclair was uncomfortable with improvisation, and was soon augmented by and then replaced by Dave MacRae (who would much later and very briefly be a member of Soft Machine).

The band recorded two fascinating studio albums and lasted in fits of aimlessness until a humiliating tour of Holland and Belgium in September 1972, for which it acted as support for the Softs. You don't cock a snook at your former bandmates when you're second on the bill. At the end of the tour, Wyatt packed up his kit and, with it, the band and, for that matter, more or less his career as a drummer. A drunken fall the following June left him paraplegic, but what should have been his greatest grief of all saw instead the beginnings of a remarkable renaissance. In spring 1974, he worked material that had once been intended for a third Matching Mole album into new structures and compositions to create *Rock Bottom* – and there has surely never been another album that so brilliantly matches adversity with artistic triumph.

Fourth (1971)

Personnel:
Roy Babbington: acoustic bass
Mark Charig: cornet
Elton Dean: alto saxophone, saxello
Nick Evans: trombone
Jimmy Hastings: flute, bass clarinet
Hugh Hopper: bass
Mike Ratledge: keyboards
Alan Skidmore: tenor saxophone
Robert Wyatt: drums
Recorded October–November 1970, Olympic Studios, London, UK
Producer: Soft Machine
Label: CBS
Release date: February 1971
Running time: 39:01 (A: 18:47, B: 20:14)

Despite the album's wraparound image, it was never released as a gatefold. It was titled *Fourth* in all territories. No bonus tracks have ever been released.

'Teeth' (Ratledge)

To the various mooted origins of the title – gritted teeth, Hell's teeth, lying through your teeth, play it by the skin of one's teeth, and so on – I'm tempted to add one more: Conrad Poohs and His Amazing Dancing Teeth, a Terry Gilliam animation set to a jaunty carnival organ in an episode of *Monty Python's Flying Circus*. Unfortunately, it aired on 1 December 1970, shortly after the recording of the album had finished. But that doesn't entirely invalidate it, and neither do live performances of the piece in November, which would absolutely not have been announced on stage. It's tempting for two reasons. First, the absurdity would have appealed to a band that would later record 'Stanley Stamps Gibbon Album'. And second, we sure do need some of that Soft Machine levity on *Fourth*, an album that is otherwise entirely humourless.

From its opening seconds, 'Teeth' spins us somewhere new. We don't hear any of the familiar trio or even Dean's sax blast. We hear Roy Babbington's double bass, heralding not jazz rock but electric bebop: a series of John Coltrane-style variations that squall and stutter for more than a minute before finally picking up a rhythm. Notably, Ratledge has scaled back the organ abuse in favour of spritely electric piano lines, and with Babbington's melodic bass playing, there's not a whiff of Hopper's fuzz. Seemingly in reaction to the more delicate beat, Wyatt returns to what was so lacking on *Third*, his tumbling rounds of fills that propel Dean's weaving, shapeshifting sax.

A second Babbington feature at 3:10 drives the piece into a hard-nosed section of old-style Soft Machine theatrics on a massed brass and winds section that plays as if struggling to remain upright on the deck of a storm-pitched ship that might capsize at any moment. From 4:55, the front liners attempt slabs of ensemble blowing against a frenetic Ratledge organ solo. At 8:00, all this is flung aside for a flittering coda of feverish chaos that ends unresolved with Babbington mangling the remains of his bass.

Wild, punching, and so tightly and meticulously plotted that it seems to contain more ideas than the band's entire catalogue before it, 'Teeth' suggests an exhilarating future: *Volume Two*-style intensity ramped up still further so that the listener either clings on or is tossed aside. But the very fact that it exhausted everything Ratledge had written for the album in just nine minutes made it untenable. Whereas – on paper at least – the organist's compositions had dominated *Third*, 'Teeth' was his only credit on *Fourth*, and his shortest orphan piece to that point.

Frank Zappa could have handled the creative onslaught, and did so on *Waka/Jawaka* and *The Grand Wazoo* the following year, both surely inspired by this piece. But Soft Machine *couldn't* handle it, and so the rest of the album is a retreat.

'Kings And Queens' (Hopper)

For running time alone, it's Hopper who dominates *Fourth*, with this five-minute piece the lesser of his contributions. It's based on one of the album's recurring sonic motifs: the swells of Ratledge's electric piano. Hopper adds a languorous bass part, Wyatt's playing is busy but becalmed, and a front line of Dean, Mark Charig, and Nick Evans entwine in surf-speckled stillness. The piece is beautiful but transient, slipping past like the thoughts of a stoned listener – achingly important in the moment, forgotten the instant they're enunciated.

'Fletcher's Blemish' (Dean)

The others were kind to give Dean space on the album, but who wouldn't have preferred something by Wyatt here? The – album's shortest track (4:33) – sets out the same stall of misshapen but intriguing pottery that Dean would record for his first solo album. Babbington's bass features again, and is distressed from the start. Then Dean and Charig blast into the ugliest Soft Machine theme to date, a stop/start concatenation of random body parts and the motorway pile-up sloppings hosed to the hard shoulder. Ratledge interjects his swells, Wyatt thunders, and Hopper finds places for fuzz-laced Tourette's, but in tipping the balance from structured lines to free blowing, Dean has crossed a band Rubicon. Before 'Fletcher's Blemish', this kind of thing was reserved for the closing meltdowns of longer works. With nothing to attach to, the piece seems like filler for the sake of it.

'Virtually Part 1' (Hopper)

Soft Machine had always played long pieces but had rarely designed them in defined structures, a legacy of those early days when suites were built simply by connecting whatever would fit. A repeated theme is all that hangs 'Rivmic Melodies' together, and small repeated phrases are the only unifiers in three of the zigzagging pieces on *Third*. The fourth, 'Moon In June', lacks them altogether, and is more obviously just an assemblage of parts.

Hopper's second and last grand piece for the band continues this way of working, but occupies a strange hybrid space. 'Virtually' is a side-long suite like those of *Third*, but is presented as four individual tracks. There's no return to the head.

A near-silence between parts 2 and 3 ought to invalidate it as a single track, but there was also silence in the middle of 'Out-Bloody-Rageous', so it doesn't. Given what we know of him, we can't typify Hopper's working practices – he wasn't responsible for 'Rivmic Melodies', and 'Facelift' was a tape work based on a piece that had become extended on stage – but we *can* assume that 'Virtually' is a piecemeal suite made from crudely fixing together disparate sections, and that the exercise is summarily completed the moment it reaches the 20-minute mark.

Babbington is again the opening feature, adding spice to a simple two-note fanfare. Wyatt finds ways to bring the foot-dragging theme to life, leaning heavily on cymbal patter and abrupt tom runs. The bulk of the piece consists of Babbington's inventive reframing of the theme. He seems to be the only thing moving. Ratledge does no more than play the chords over and over, but he's the anchor for the 7/8 rhythm, permission for the others to play free – an inversion of his usual role as featured soloist.

'Virtually Part 2' (Hopper)

An abrupt herald on brass switches straight into this long, mostly rhythmless feature for fuzz organ. Dean's saxello loosely follows his lines, occasionally dropping into unison, while Hopper and Wyatt entangle each other in counterpoints. At 8:50, we're back into Ratledge's alternating electric piano chords in 7/8, over which Dean blows and Hopper tries out different configurations of his own theme. Wyatt simply puts his head down to pummel his kit. The piece comes to an abrupt halt at 12:18, and with it, the last of the rock contingent of the side's jazz rock.

'Virtually Part 3' (Hopper)

Hopper is back in tape mode here, layering random forwards-and-backwards sax lines over a skittering backwards organ/drum rhythm that recalls the opening of 'Out-Bloody-Rageous'. (This rhythm is Wyatt's only appearance in the section.) At 12:44, the tapes are replaced by electric bass, over which Dean and Alan Skidmore's saxes and Jimmy Hastings's clarinet braid random lines. Hopper's lumbering improvised fuzz and Ratledge's subtle, glowing swells take over from 14:15, again with Dean finding ways to respond to the motifs, an interaction that continues to the end of the section at 16:56.

'Virtually Part 4' (Hopper)

More swells, clean bass, and gradually accumulating electric piano lines move the listener through an acreage even more horizontal than the last. Toward the end, Wyatt's barely audible mallet fills and Ratledge's chords build tension that the band make no attempt to resolve. The suite ends disappointingly on a fade.

Was 'Virtually' a failed experiment? Yes, it failed. And no, it wasn't really an experiment since there's little here of the questing studio manipulation that characterises the best of Hopper's solo work. There are plenty of textures, but that short tape sequence in 'Part 3' seems to be the only moment that Hopper took the same care here as he had in 'Facelift'.

Naturally, the proof of any pudding is in the eating. *Fourth* was a success. Those who bought it on the back of *Third* surely understood that a Soft Machine album takes time and effort to assimilate, and were, therefore willing to buy it essentially untested. It would grow on them with more playing. But many of those purchasers didn't follow the band forward into *Fifth* – hence, we can assume that what they found they considered to be stodgy, a little flavourless, and not at all nourishing.

The Post-Wyatt Quartets

It feels like another ending, and for many fans of early Soft Machine this is where they bail. Even *Fourth* is an album too many for some – a sudden loss of emotional connection that had been encapsulated in Wyatt's voice and the image (even if you couldn't see him) of a sweaty, half-bare man hunched over his drums with his hair in his face. Without him, the others became all but anonymous. There are no front-cover group shots on UK releases for five long years after *Fourth*, simply a sequence of largely characterless and somewhat disagreeable designs. All *Fifth* had to offer was the number.

The band *did* have virtuosos in the future, in particular the guitarists Allan Holdsworth and John Etheridge. Significantly, it's with them that the band finally ditched their album-title numbering. The numbering had worked for Chicago, whose similarly faceless image was based on clever artistic manipulations of a curvy, appealing, and instantly recognisable logo. For Soft Machine, the numbers seemed to suggest a constant progression, as if each album was a journal entry. But progression only works if it keeps heading forwards. The general criticism levelled at Soft Machine by those abandoning them at this point is that everything after *Fourth* was a contraction into an unadventurous establishment space, and that the band actively abandoned experimentation in favour of increasingly formal jazz.

For sure, the diehards kept the band alive, as diehards do. For many prog rock fans, Soft Machine were the only jazz group they allowed into their collections. But we are passing now pass the age of their legend, and we won't view the post-Wyatt band through the same thrilling lens as the earlier incarnations. The bulk of every Soft Machine biography is now behind us.

Suddenly, everything they do seems so much less significant – the main reason being their ongoing lack of success. Commercially, *Third* was the high point. Artistically, many critics also laud *Third* over the others, while fans might even plump for *Volume Two*. Had the band made either a commercial or artistic breakthrough post-Wyatt, then the story would be completely different. We might even think of them as Yes after Bill Bruford, or Genesis after Peter Gabriel, or the various flavours of King Crimson. Instead, we have a slow decline until 1978 when Soft Machine ceased making music altogether – not because they had nothing more to say, but because they could no longer afford the studio time. Younger, hungrier bands were commanding the advances.

The albums were still good. That's not the issue. But, like Pierre Moerlen's Gong trying to claim an audience post-Daevid Allen, a hefty shadow hung over the post-Wyatt Soft Machine, and being adept is not enough to bring light into that dark place. Fusion itself rose and fell almost as swiftly as prog rock, which was largely exhausted by 1974. To survive, you needed something that would spark a new generation of fans, and Soft Machine didn't have it. Even an album as fresh as *Softs* largely fell by the wayside. It seemed that every bedsit in Britain had a copy of that album in the early 1980s, filed right next to Gong's *Gazeuse!*. The greater world ignored it.

The hard truth is that nobody within Soft Machine was particularly happy with the band either. They seemed to keep going mainly out of inertia. The name still had cachet and could still fill halls. With time ticking precariously away, and no prospects as good as the parent band, you played it safe for as long as you could.

Can you envision Hopper and Ratledge holding a party in September 1971, with dancing girls and streamers? They should have been elated that the troublesome Wyatt was finally out of the frame. It's likely that they couldn't have actively fired him themselves – he was that most sacred of things, an *original member* – but he'd been a gloomy presence in the band for far too long. A new drummer would bring stability and a shift of focus to musicianship and composition. There was even an obvious candidate: Dean's colleague Phil Howard, who'd played with them in March for the BBC. They'd soon be back in the dressing room, bonding over their chess and crosswords.

Their prospects should have been bright. The band should have spiralled upwards. But you can't envision that *party*, can you?

Instead, Hopper and Ratledge swerved from one crisis to another. This time, Howard's arrival shifted the power structure somewhere it had never been before: to two equal and incompatible factions. Dean and Howard wanted the band to move further into free-blowing. Hopper and Ratledge wanted to move further into notated chamber jazz. The former thought a rhythm was a malleable thing, part of the creative elation of the moment. The latter thought it should be a tightly regulated tempo on which they could build their extemporisations.

The latter pair had superiority and dealt with the issue in the simplest way. Howard was excised within four months, leaving as his official legacy one live release, one more BBC session, and half of the new album. But this only caused further conflict since the decision was effectively also a rebuke against Dean.

The live release is *Drop* (2008), recorded at the Berliner Jazztage '71 in the Philharmoniehalle, West Berlin, on 7 November 1971. Just look at the dynamic in that pool-playing cover photo. Howard's looning, Dean's laughing along, Hopper seems half amused and half discomforted, and Ratledge just wants to be somewhere else.

The set begins with an unofficial manifesto for the blowing pair, 'Neo-Caliban Grides'. From the opening seconds, Howard slams at his kit as if he's wielding hammers, Dean wails manically alongside him, and Hopper and Ratledge are left somewhere in the wake, trying to anchor themselves into the spectre of structure. All right, but that's 'Neo-Caliban Grides' – we know that's how it sounds. But it's followed by Ratledge's 'All White', one of five tracks tonight destined for *Fifth*, and the feel is identical. Howard thunders, Dean squalls, the others hang on to their tails. And so it's repeated with 'Drop', 'M.C.', and 'As If', like a goat in a tumble dryer.

And then there are the oldies – 'Slightly All The Time', 'Out-Bloody-Rageous', and 'Pigling Bland' – and nothing's changed. Howard attacks every surface in sight, punctuating his barrage with disconcerting thumps at his twin bass drums. Dean threads disconnected runs of electric piano. Ratledge seems uncertain how to integrate his Lowrey, and Hopper's attempts to follow the original version's foundation lines are largely ignored.

Howard may well be one of those jazz and rock powerhouses that rose so explosively in the 1970s (think Shuggie Otis, Jaco Pastorius, or Randy Rhoads), but it's hard to believe he's actually listening to the ensemble here, and not just providing gleeful accompaniment to the noise in his head. This is *not* about a master craftsman daring his collaborators to up their game. This is someone who just wants to dominate the frequencies. Listening to *Drop* is like fighting to hear a respectable jazz trio play in a hurricane. Sure, there's the excitement and the danger, but you wish to hell the wind would relent once in a while.

The surviving BBC session was recorded eight days later in London's Playhouse Theatre. (A session for *Sound Of The 70s* at Kensington House the following day seems to have vanished without trace.) Three tracks were played: 'As If', 'Drop', and the ten-minute improvisation 'Welcome To Frillsville'. All are available on *BBC Radio 1971–1974* (2003). They're exactly what you'd expect: a near-indistinguishable tumult of free playing dominated by Howard's churning runs with Ratledge's themes bolted awkwardly onto the ends. There's a point toward the end of 'Frillsville' where you think it's about to settle, but Howard won't allow it.

That the drummer galvanised Soft Machine is undeniable. But he also steered them into an artistic *cul-de-sac*. There would be nowhere left to take the band, no hope for new Ratledge or Hopper compositions if all that could be expected was bluster, and no room for the subtlety that bruised fans would surely demand after a couple of releases with this kind of onslaught.

Howard was purged after the first run of *Fifth* sessions, six days in November and December. To replace him, Hopper and Ratledge turned to John Marshall, who'd actually been their first choice back in September but was too busy at the time. Marshall had a significant history. He'd played on Graham Collier's first two studio albums, *Deep Dark Blue Centre* and *Down Another Road*, alongside woodwind player Karl Jenkins. Marshall and Jenkins then joined Ian Carr in his jazz-rock supergroup Nucleus, and were present on that band's peak releases – *Elastic Rock* (1970), *We'll Talk About It Later*, and *Solar Plexus* (both 1971) – all essential adjuncts to the Soft Machine sound and if anything more questing, since they also amalgamated aspects of pure rock, blues, and funk. As a session drummer, Marshall had played alongside Ray Russell on Bill Fay's eponymous first album, and been in the crowds that recorded Michael Gibbs's first and *Tanglewood 63*, Neil Ardley's *Greek Variations & Other Aegean Exercises*, Centipede's *Septober Energy*, and the Chitinous Ensemble's magnificent *Chitinous*. When he first got the call,

Marshall had been supporting Jack Bruce's *Harmony Row* in a trio with the ever-present Chris Spedding. In February 1972, he shifted to Soft Machine in time for the five days of sessions that provided the second half of *Fifth*.

Marshall was a tonic to the world's grumpiest jazz band. He relaxed both the drum parts *and* the atmosphere. But it wouldn't be Soft Machine without tension, and this time it was Dean who was the outsider. Dean's unhappiness with the power-play that had flung Howard from the band escalated into a commitment to leave.

Aside from *Fifth*, we have only one official record of the quartet with Dean and Marshall. On May 2 – the first date of a two-week tour of France that would be Dean's scheduled finale – Europe 1 radio broadcast a live set at Paris's Olympia music hall. This was released in 1995 as *Live In France*, and reissued in 2004 under the title *Live In Paris May 2nd, 1972*. The improvisations are smoother, more contemplative, less defiantly out. And though Marshall's no slouch with the fills, he leaves plenty of room for the others. 'Slightly All The Time' slinks in back-alley curls, leading the listener on a circuitous but ultimately fruitless midnight meander like 1970s kids chasing the rumour of drugs. 'Out-Bloody-Rageous' infuses the senses like a consoling cup of camomile tea back in mum's kitchen. Even 'Facelift' has swapped its abusive introduction for shimmering ripples of duetting electric pianos. Ratledge has equipped himself with a new organ and leans on the most genteel of its settings like this is early Caravan or a rehearsal for Hatfield And The North, and Hopper has switched off his fuzz. You can feel both the disappointment of the free-noise crowd, who might have thought Soft Machine would become rock's version of Alan Silva, and the complex bipolarity of those who knew by 1972 the Actuel free-noise roster was a dead end but didn't quite comprehend how far fusion needed to backtrack before it was safely on the road again.

For the players, too, this surely seemed like a trap. Hopper and Ratledge were edging toward their own disconnect – fewer compositions, more coasting – and seemed willing to subsume their own band vision, whatever that might be (and by 1972, we surely had no idea), to that of a stronger personality. One that arrived on cue as Dean's replacement in the form of Karl Jenkins.

Among other benefits, Jenkins was a multi-instrumentalist capable of reproducing Dean's roles as front-line soloist and keyboard foil. He'd proven himself as a session player on everything from Elton John's *Tumbleweed Connection* (oboe) to the original LP version of *Jesus Christ Superstar* (piano). You'll find Jenkins in many of the same scenes as Carr and Marshall. He was also a prolific composer. Nucleus may ostensibly been Carr's band, but Jenkins wrote the majority of their first two albums. He also knew how to assume control, having largely written, performed on, and orchestrated Affinity singer Linda Hoyle's first solo album *Pieces Of Me*. He'd even joined Soft Machine on stage in the Wyatt period, playing Ratledge's Hohner.

Jenkins's drawback – one that escalated as he took on an ever more central role in the band – was his antipathy towards rock. But it's wrong to complain that he swerved the band into establishment jazz. *Live In France* reveals that the process was already well-advanced before he joined. However, Jenkins rubbed people the wrong way – not the least, fans. Hopper certainly had no truck with him, and was now sidling toward the door.

Within days of him joining the band, Jenkins's integration was demonstrated to the world. On 11 July, Soft Machine returned to Maida Vale for another BBC session, part of which is available on *BBC Radio 1971–1974* (it's not from 11 April, as the liner notes claim). Not only is Jenkins on the 11-minute sequence that was released, but he even wrote its opening theme, 'Fanfare', which was later to open *Six*. The rest is an abbreviation of side one of *Fifth*, demonstrating Jenkins's prowess on oboe and saxes. In contrast to Dean, Jenkins tends to play melodic runs: lilting tunes composed in the moment rather than flurries of wild fingering. A second sequence, consisting of 'Stumble' (another Jenkins number destined for *Six*), 'L B O', and 'As If', seems not to have survived.

Largely the same set was taken to the Paris Theatre nine days later for an *In Concert* performance best heard as *Softstage BBC In Concert 1972* (2005). Except for 'Slightly All The Time', here calm and especially beautiful when Jenkins unwinds the melody on oboe, the set consists of material from *Fifth* and a handful of tracks destined for *Six*. Pointedly, even at this early stage, the new pieces are mostly Jenkins compositions: his feature 'Fanfare' and the complex funky lines and time signatures of 'Stumble' and 'Riff'. There's only one new Ratledge piece, 'Gesolreut', and nothing from Hopper.

Indeed, the period saw Hopper's slow divorce inch toward the paperwork. He was friendless, bored, and creatively stagnant, though he did manage to find an outlet in the solo album *1984*, which in turn gave him a somewhat forlorn platform to inject radicalism back into Soft Machine.

Two further BBC sessions for *Sounds Of The 70s* and *Full House* in October and December have never been officially released, and there are no standalone live releases for a full year after *Softstage*. However, YouTube has part of a rebroadcast of the *Full House* TV transmission of 'Fanfare' and 'All White', and footage of the band on 6 August, a wall of grizzly moustaches, soundchecking the same sequence on French TV, including Jenkins handling a baritone sax almost as big as he is. But in October and November, the band recorded gigs at Brighton and Guildford for use as the first disc of *Six*, and they spent most of the rest of the year on the studio half.

The gap masks Hopper's spiral into a state very similar to that Wyatt had experienced before him. By the time Hopper finally left in April 1973, it seemed as if none of the others even noticed his passing. The last gasp of a long and significant tenure (at least for the time being) was appearing as a guest for the band's set at Congresszentrum, Hamburg, on 17 May. This was recorded for West German TV and eventually released as the 2010 CD/DVD set

NDR Jazz Workshop. Hopper may be relegated to second bassist and part of an extended group including guitarist Gary Boyle and saxophonist Art Themen, but at least he got to manipulate his '1983' tapes live for a full 15 minutes even if (sadly) there's no visual evidence and most of the audio channels didn't record properly. The concert also saw Soft Machine back a short, troubled set by Linda Hoyle, but that's not on the release in either format.

The *real* bassist for the set was Hopper's replacement Roy Babbington, who'd played acoustic bass on *Fourth* and *Fifth* and now shifted to 6-string electric. Babbington had also found himself in Nucleus for a while, playing on *Labyrinth* (1973) and Ian Carr's solo album *Belladonna* (1972), where the sessions also included Allan Holdsworth. These are two more highly recommended recordings. Babbington had also played on Mike Cooper's *Trout Steel*, Keith Tippett's *Blueprint*, and the 1973 Ovary Lodge album, among many others, and been part of Delivery – alongside Phil Miller, Pip Pyle, Lol Coxhill, and pianist Steve Miller – including on their album *Fools Meeting* (1970). Unlike Hopper's starchy lines, Babbington valued the groove, and played exactly the kind of funk rhythms that Jenkins was writing for.

NDR is a beautifully presented piece: part gig, part showcase, up-front in studio-vivid detail and revealing a band whose gear had significantly improved since the Bremen *Beat-Club* footage of two years earlier. Ratledge, in particular, is surrounded by keys and electronics, while Jenkins has his own elaborate setup, including Ratledge's cast-off Hohner on top of his Rhodes. Marshall's kit includes bells, chimes, triangle, gong, and other paraphernalia.

Almost the entire set is from *Six* – the one major exception is 'Down The Road', a funky Jenkins number soon to be recorded for *Seven*. Unsurprisingly, the primary focus in the first half is on Jenkins as he dances through his arsenal of woods and leaps repeatedly on the electric piano. In the second half, Themen is a shapeless saxophonist of the Dean school, while Boyle mostly limits himself to rhythm. The highlight is 'Chloe And The Pirates', where a solo Ratledge plays Rhodes through an Echoplex to soft tape backing. The band seeps in softly behind him, and if only Themen could have controlled himself, the piece would be perfection. He can't, so Ratledge chooses to look the other way throughout, toward Jenkins's more sympathetic counterpoint. Boyle finally gets to solo on 'Gesolreut', revealing an adept and slightly dirty jazz voice that is most certainly the shape of things to come.

Later that May, parts of the Babbington quartet's performance at the Bataclan in Paris were recorded for the TV program *Pop 2*. You can see them on YouTube. The highlight is Jenkins's tenor recorder solo during 'Down The Road'.

In July, the band recorded *Seven* using what little money was left from the CBS deal, and returned to the BBC on 30 October for a session to promote the album's release. You can hear all four pieces on *BBC Radio 1971–1974*. Perversely, only 'Down The Road' is actually from *Seven*. 'Stanley Stamp's Gibbon Album' looks backwards, while a brief version of Jenkins's 'Hazard

Profile' looks ahead. Babbington's fuzz-bass workout 'Sinepost' appears to be merely another short link like the ones littered throughout *NDR*.

Much more of the same snapshot in time is available on a good quality audience recording of a gig four days earlier at De Lantaren, Rotterdam, released officially in 2023 as *The Dutch Lesson*. Despite the *Seven*-referencing title, again only 'Down The Road' comes from the album. The bulk of the set is a rendition of much of *Six* played by a band comfortable enough with each other to stretch out on almost every piece. There are particularly long and effective versions of 'The Soft Weed Factor' and 'Chloe And The Pirates'. Of the other work, 'Ealing Comedy' is an entertaining five-minute bass solo, and the still-embryonic 'Hazard Profile' stretched to 19 enthralling minutes of jamming and improvisation.

There were two more significant performances this year. On 4 November, the band played two shows at London's Rainbow Theatre, supporting the newly stratospheric Pink Floyd to raise money for Robert Wyatt. The shows did their job, but neither band's sets have been released officially. Then, at the end of the month, Ratledge and Jenkins joined Mick Taylor, Steve Hillage, Fred Frith, Pierre Moerlen, and many more, to back another stratospheric success, Mike Oldfield, on a version of side one of *Tubular Bells* filmed for the BBC's *2nd House*. The footage is best obtained as part of the 2009 *Tubular Bells* deluxe edition. Ratledge stays in the shadows, but Jenkins's oboe feature is a treat.

Including Boyle on parts of the NDR performance could be seen as a rehearsal for what happened next, or maybe it was all those great stylists on the *Tubular Bells* film. In December, the quartet added a fifth member: the band's first undeniable full-time guitarist since 1967 and one a world away from his predecessor.

Fifth (1972)

Personnel:
Roy Babbington: acoustic bass
Elton Dean: alto saxophone, saxello, electric piano
Hugh Hopper: bass
Phil Howard: drums (side 1)
John Marshall: drums (side 2)
Mike Ratledge: keyboards
Recorded November 1971–February 1972, Advision Studios, London, UK
Producer: Soft Machine
Label: CBS
Release date: June 1972
Running time: 36:32 (A: 18:44, B: 17:48)

The album was known as *Soft Machine Fifth* in the UK and *Soft Machine 5* in North America, with slightly different covers. It had equally confusing titles in other territories – *Soft Machine Fifth* (the Netherlands), *Fifth* (France), *5* (Italy), and *Soft Machine Cinco* (Spain). Though 'Bone' is included on all releases, it wasn't listed on the original European editions. The 2004 Sony CD added the bonus track 'All White (Take Two)', which has become standard on the format ever since.

'All White' (Ratledge)
Only Dean's saxello playing marks the opening as jazz. On guitar, organ, or even piano or vibes, this could still be rock. It's a lovely moment of calm – a dancer's movements in near darkness, with only Hopper's clean, isolated notes to ground the gravity-defying, reverb-vaulted flights. But from 1:41, the mood shifts. Phil Howard is a harsher, more assertive drummer than Wyatt, and the sound is more boxy and less forgiving. The result is a frostier version of Ratledge's familiar simple 7/8 riffs, a group that has turned from airless suspension to the confinement signalled by the title's musical restriction. The quality of Dean's blowing is never in doubt, but for the bulk of the six minutes of 'All White' that's all it has: Dean featuring against a jabbing rhythm section that seems unsettled but is actually thoroughly conventional.

'Drop' (Ratledge)
Essentially, this track is a repeat of the previous track's dichotomy. We're first immersed in the cavernous liquid space that gives it the title, where electric piano imitations of sprinkling water converge into hovering cycles of forward and backward loops at various speeds – that whole 'Out-Bloody-Rageous' thing again. Then, two minutes in, Ratledge adds more assertive melody fragments and the band settles behind him: Hopper in crisp runs and patterns, Dean on soft refractions of electric piano riffs, Howard propelling

from the front. The feature this time is Ratledge's thin-lipped organ playing moving at desperate speed across a skittery rhythm that you won't be surprised to hear is in 7/8 yet again.

'M. C.' (Hopper)

Hopper – once star of the show – manages only this filler on *Fifth*, and like Dean's contribution to *Fourth,* it's an interval for free playing. Howard takes the opening, again treated to a shiny-wall sheen of echo, while Ratledge's electric piano and Dean's saxes nudge tentatively at uncomfortable corners. But the difference between 'M.C.' and the earlier tracks is that it never shifts into a second half. It feels like it's building to a grand entrance that never arrives. Instead, it simply rolls away just as it came in, like a fifth part to 'Virtually' still in search of closure.

'As If' (Ratledge)

The album's most substantial track (7:55) would go on to enjoy one of the longest performance careers of any Soft Machine piece. For side two, new player John Marshall takes over on drums and guest Roy Babbington is back on upright bass, fomenting a sound that is both breathtaking in its ability and made of granite-hewn jazz chops.

Thundering drum salvos and massed Dean saxes seem to announce just how uncompromising the piece intends to be, only for Ratledge to defy expectations with another brooding, sinewy electric piano section (in a surprisingly manageable 4/4, 4/4, 3/4) over Hopper's midnight creep and Dean's sax phrases on the very brink of breath hiss. From about 3:34, Babbington's string-coil ratchets add a distressing spectral undercurrent, and when his bass begins to shadow, deepen, and then totally subsume the bass part half a minute later, it's with a coal cellar nightmare of spidery intelligence that soon becomes the piece's dominant mood. The rest is the slow collapse of a gutted body that takes forever to hit the floor in a series of bone-cracking impacts whose shock lines you can see travelling in slow motion through the insensible flesh.

'L B O' (Marshall)

Erupting from the tail of 'As If', 'L B O' is two minutes of Marshall's drumming punctuated by manic sax and organ bleats. If that doesn't excite you, the idea that the title might be a poor phonetic reading of the word 'elbow' isn't going to make the track more palatable.

'Pigling Bland' (Ratledge)

This new setting of an older composition continues side two's quasi-suite (in which all the tracks segue) with a swerve back into the languor of 'As If' alternating with short up-tempo stretches like a compressed day in the life of a manic depressive. There's bluesy resignation in the slow sections, a bright false smile in the fast. Ratledge is on electric piano throughout, and Dean weeps and cavorts repeatedly as appropriate. A sudden swipe into a fast, helter-skeltering section at 3:34 adds a little more nostalgia. These unpredictable inversions are what Soft Machine *used* to do. It remains in carnivalesque good spirits for the remaining 49 seconds, ending on a pummelling evocation of the 'Esther's Nose Job' suite.

'Bone' (Dean)

Dean's back driving for the second time here, and the question is whether we can end *both* sides of *Fifth* with free skronk. Actually, it's the disc's greatest surprise: a thrumming three-minute soundscape in which an insectile organ busies itself among jungle blooms to a backdrop of whistling foliage, exotic bird calls, and distant howler monkey reverberations.

'All White (Take Two)' (Ratledge)

This take is quite different to the one used on the album. Dean's saxello introduction is entirely missing, replaced by a Howard drum feature. Howard is fierce but without finesse, pumping at the skins in rounds that give little room for the others, and he keeps it up to the last second. Hopper reacts by playing circular variations of his patterns and Ratledge adds frustrated clusters of electric piano. It's easier to hear here (rather than on Howard's side of the album proper) that Dean feeds inspiration off the drummer, reacting to the rhythm fragments with manic runs. The others might as well not be there.

Six (1973)

Personnel:
Hugh Hopper: bass
Karl Jenkins: oboe, saxophones, keyboards
John Marshall: drums
Mike Ratledge: keyboards
Recorded: Live disc at Brighton, 20 October 1972 and Guildford, 1 November 1972. Studio disc November–December 1972, CBS Studios, London, UK – except '1983', Advision, London
Producer: Soft Machine
Label: CBS
Release date: February 1973
Running time: 1:16:25 (A: 19:21, B: 22:27, C: 17:14, D: 17:23)

The band's second double album was always presented as a live LP and a studio LP packaged together. In the UK and US, each disc had a side one and side two – the US version with different catalogue numbers. It was *Six* in all territories. Like *Third*, it was able to fit on a single CD, so it has never suffered amputations. No bonus tracks have ever been released.

'Fanfare' (Jenkins)
Something is surely awry when the band that once gave us 'Hibou Anemone and Bear' and 'Esther's Nose Job' starts labelling tracks 'Fanfare', 'Between', and 'Riff'. But 'Fanfare' delivers what's required of it in its 42 seconds: the arrival of Karl Jenkins (soon-to-be band superstar), and the first Soft Machine album solely recorded by the current members of the band.

Like notable live/studio double albums before it – Cream's *Wheels Of Fire*, Pentangle's *Sweet Child*, Pink Floyd's *Ummagumma*, The Byrds' *(Untitled)*, and so on – it's as if the album is a declaration of the entire compass of the band's abilities in all the forums available to it. And, incredibly, there's practically no looking backwards. All but one of the tracks is brand new. Moreover, as a statement of band invention, it offers a vision of collective and individual strength.

The live album is presented the old-fashioned Soft Machine way, as one complete suite of unbroken music on each side, where egos collapse into a unified group sound. The studio tracks are separate showcases for Jenkins, Ratledge, and Hopper – quite literally in the last case – and we can rue the lack of a John Marshall piece to make the conceit perfect. Still, we know full well what it would have sounded like.

Pompous, ridiculously inflated, and as cocksure as a jazz-fusion Led Zeppelin, 'Fanfare' enables each musician to insert himself into the musical mix: Jenkins's swaggering sax theme, swirling up-and-down highlights on Ratledge's electric piano, argumentative interruptions from Marshall's kit, and Hopper's bass, heavy as a dragged anchor to prevent the showboaters

85

pulling the music back into free jazz. It adds up to true danger we've sorely missed and a sense of gritted-teeth endurance we'll never hear again.

'All White' (Ratledge)
The lilting 7/8 beat may be familiar, but Jenkins's oboe swerves the one old piece into a new, tremulous space poised somewhere in that long dusty stretch between Morocco and India where hobbled camels foxtrot ganglingly. The others give him immense space for his sidewinder extemporisations, and a surely tacked-on audience finds space to interject Soft Machine's first official recognition that they're playing for more than themselves.

'Between' (Jenkins, Ratledge)
This long bridge appears to be an improvisation for dual electric pianos, assisted by softly pattering bass and diffuse, heat-shimmering percussion. The two keyboardists seem fully comfortable with each other, tossing joyous spirals to each other across the stage.

'Riff' (Jenkins)
Hopper picks up the makings of the theme and Marshall immediately falls in behind him, weaving through the first of Jenkins's tangled knots of torturous, lumpy rhythms. Jenkins lays down a bed of electric piano to help the others navigate, leaving Ratledge to slop and skitter all over the top in one of his last great organ eruptions.

'37½' (Ratledge)
After four minutes, the band collapses, leaving Hopper to wend his way through a brief passage of riff fragments. Out of this coalesces a surprising Gong-style 'have a cup of tea' funk vamp – though it has to be said, with none of that band's stoned ease – above which Jenkins takes a series of solos on sax and oboe. The fade is disappointing, but the track caps the band's best album side in years.

'Gesolreut' (Ratledge)
No such luck, Grateful Dead aficionados: side two doesn't fade back in where side one left off. 'Gesolreut' (an early reading form for those who don't know notation, a sort of Medieval do-re-mi) punches in on Ratledge's electric piano with no sense of being in a live venue at all. The funk is even more pronounced, despite the undanceable rhythm, with a humorous full-throated sax and electric piano theme that defies you not to try to throw jerky shapes to it. The long solo section is at least in a manageable 6/4 rhythm.

'E.P.V.' (Jenkins)
Ratledge's electric piano shimmers and Jenkins's oboe wavers in a depthless trance space. It's haunting, oceanic, and sexy. Gradually, it gathers

propulsion, only to let it slide deliciously away into the clutches of yet another dream state. The title alone belays the reverie, being simply the initials of a colleague's relative and hence of no worth whatsoever.

'Lefty' (Hopper, Jenkins, Marshall, Ratledge)
An altogether chillier vibe (possibly the sinister reading of the title) pushes the unwary into one of the few pieces ever credited to the band collectively. It's a free improvisation sounding like nothing so much as the accumulated montage of a thousand bedroom doors slamming in your face.

'Stumble' (Jenkins)
'Lefty' eventually coheres into this brief mock-triumphant keyboards theme. A well-composed variation prevents the repeated iterations of the motif from driving you crazy, but at the same time, you know full well where this is leading ...

'5 From 13 (For Phil Seamen With Love And Thanks)' (Marshall)
... which is into another John Marshall drum feature, this time filling a whole five minutes. British jazz drummer Phil Seamen had died exactly a week before the Brighton gig. Rock fans will probably know him best from a stint with Ginger Baker's Air Force, but you'll find him on a huge range of 1960s jazz and R&B recordings.

'Riff II' (Jenkins)
This is a variation on the broken-backed 'Riff' groove played in fierce unison for 46 seconds, followed by a stomping audience that brays for more.

'The Soft Weed Factor' (Jenkins)
All four tracks on the studio disc are fascinating indicators of the band's future, though Hopper's was clearly the longshot. Surely, the money was still on Ratledge – the venerable patrician of the band's shifting commune – whose creativity might have slipped markedly since *Third* but who still might shepherd the others into a new generation of driving, inventive, quick-changing rock. It's notable then that Jenkins is first out of the stalls, and with the set's longest track (11:17), and that by co-opting the magic word 'Soft' it all but shrieks its claim of legitimacy.
The title is actually a reference to Ebenezer Cooke's 1708 poem 'The Sot-Weed Factor', but like Soft Machine's other adoptions of literary titles at the time, that's the only connection. Sot-weed is nothing stronger than tobacco. But it does indicate Jenkins's regard for centuries-old poetry, which would eventually lead to *Land Of Cockayne* (1981).
We've heard minimalism from the band before, in Ratledge's tape loop sections on 'Out-Bloody-Rageous', but nothing quite as calm, elegant, and mesmeric as this. For more than a minute, Jenkins's feathery electric piano

riff, in simple strolling 4/4 time, is the only thing moving in the right channel, and from then on there's not much more than a chiming counterpoint on the left before drum and bass finally slink in at 3:14. The oboe theme, precisely shadowed by organ, is as restrained as a hunting cat that knows it has all the time in the world to creep from one leaf to the next. Subliminal accents, mainly on Marshall's peripheral instruments, keep the track from ossifying, while Hopper's bouncy playing and Marshall's dramatic Nick Mason-style fills provide a stately drive.

Again, it feels like Gong that's coalescing here, in particular the rounds of pattering percussion that Pierre Moerlen was later to bring to that group. It just happens that Jenkins got there first, and better.

'Stanley Stamps Gibbon Album (For B.O.)' (Ratledge)

Ratledge's first exhibit is half the length of Jenkins's track but double its intensity. He even injects humour into the title, which is taken from the famous Stanley Gibbons stamp catalogues (price lists for philatelists) as mangled by the cast of the radio programme *I'm Sorry, I'll Read That Again,* for which Bill Oddie provided songs. Marshall is the link due to his work on sessions for the much-loved TV comedy show *The Goodies,* which also starred Oddie and was then at the peak of its fame.

Ratledge starts with a labyrinthine piano riff, and Hopper adds some long-overdue cataclysmal fuzz. After 33 seconds, an organ fanfare brings in Marshall on drums and congas and a frenetic Ratledge solo over that old-time (and decidedly non-Latin) 7/8. Here it remains for more than four enthralling minutes.

'Chloe And The Pirates' (Ratledge)

Ratledge's other contribution to the studio album would, like 'As If', long outlast his tenure in the band to become one of its most dependable latter-day features. Swirls of backwards electronics frame an elegant pulsing rhythm to which Jenkins adds slipstreams of oboe motifs and puddles of solo fragments. It's by far the band's most beautiful piece – the sonic opposite to all the thrashing of the first two albums and the intense sonic terrorism of 'Facelift'. But there are surprises knitted into the symmetry, including a Hopper-esque slurp of backwards tape loops at 6:28 that seems designed merely to prevent the listener from nodding off and a prickly coda to slice-and-dice psychedelicised nerve endings.

'1983' (Hopper)

Hopper's swansong is resolutely not a concluding section of 'Virtually', and is the rudest possible awakening after the glistering calm of the previous track. Its raging tonal blasts, devastating piano theatrics, percussive fractures like radiation shock lines, buzzsaw bass surgery, and scarifying loops constitute a thematic reprise of the desolate chaos of his solo album *1984.* But the stasis that fetters the piece is likely its purpose. There's no hope of forward momentum, merely the inexorable slide into the darkness in the centre of the disc.

Seven (1973)

Personnel:
Roy Babbington: electric and acoustic bass
Karl Jenkins: oboe, saxophones, recorder, electric piano, synthesizer
John Marshall: drums
Mike Ratledge: keyboards, synthesizer
Recorded July 1973, CBS Studios, London, UK
Producer: Soft Machine
Label: CBS
Release date: October 1973
Running time: 43:08 (A: 21:43, B: 21:25)

Seven had different covers in Europe and North America. The European design – a gatefold showing a drawn computer-style grid of symbols by Roslav Szaybo – is considered definitive. The American edition was a single sleeve showing the black-and-white photos from the inside spread of the European version. No bonus tracks have ever been released.

'Nettle Bed' (Jenkins)

Twelve tracks are listed for *Seven*'s generous running time, organised into four blocks of which this five-minute opener is the only singleton. It comes huffing out of the groove on great swinging bellows of Minimoog and electric piano, immediately establishing a convoluted Jenkins melodic theme onto which are layered slops of analog synth squeal and puddly VCS 3 solos. But that's about all for the composition. The riff is relentless and so overbearing it sucks all the oxygen out of the piece, and Jenkins hasn't had the time or inclination to figure out a contrasting middle section. As its dense, spiky title suggests, 'Nettle Bed' seems designed merely as a theme: a *Rubber Riff* sample in waiting.

'Carol Anne' (Jenkins)

The side's main feature – an unbroken 17-minute collage – begins with this lyrical synth ballad dedicated to Jenkins's wife. It meanders among calm bass tones, hardly rousing for almost four elegantly introverted minutes. The track lulls the listener into a pleasant reverie, and then lulls them some more, defying the expectation of the standard Soft Machine crash – all build and no edge.

'Day's Eye' (Ratledge)

'Carol Anne' is on the verge of fading away when Ratledge's barely more buoyant jazz theme burbles in, adding plump sax accents and a reedy organ solo to a languid chord progression that barely hops even at its most driving. Marshall, for one, hangs back on the fills, while Babbington's bass is all but indistinguishable from Hopper's clean tone on *Six*.

'Bone Fire' (Ratledge)

Despite the abrasive title, this short bridge hardly registers as an interruption, and merely adds a more complex chord pattern and staccato fanfare-like stabs to the rolling rhythm of 'Day's Eye'.

'Tarabos' (Ratledge)

'Bone Fire' lands the suite on a classic Ratledge fast/slow riff, onto which Jenkins melds long sax runs. The piece ends with a set of two-chord accents that finally add true excitement to the suite, though the sumptuous, perfectly mannered production resolutely refuses to allow the corpse-kicking desecration the sequence needs.

'D.I.S.' (Marshall)

A dramatic gong strike appropriately herald's Marshall's now-standard drum feature. The title refers again to Phil Seamen (see '5 From 13' on *Six*) and a witty and perhaps even true anecdote in which an inattentive Seamen pounded his gong at the wrong moment in a stage production of *West Side Story*, collapsing the performance into disarray. All eyes were on the hapless drummer. 'Dinner is served,' Seamen declared. The three-minute solo is more experimental than usual, consisting of synth-mangled percussion and tape manipulations that surge and subside without Marshall once actually attacking his skins.

'Snodland' (Jenkins)

The first suite on side two is a 13-minute Jenkins collage that builds from two minutes of humming bass drone and tinkling electric piano and percussion. Named somewhat incongruously for an undistinguished Kent town, 'Snodland' slips in and out of view with hardly a ruffle.

'Penny Hitch' (Jenkins)

Very patiently, an electric piano rhythm seeps through the foliage of 'Snodland'. The band play a languid strolling rhythm to which Jenkins adds swimming, horizontal stretches of sax poised somewhere between riff and solo. The piece's defining trick – played with infinite restraint only the once – is a sudden slam shut on two seconds of silence before resuming on majestic buzzes of oboe. It's a moment so satisfying that the rest of the section's long drift comes painted with a grin of stoned pleasure. Even starchy old Jenkins seems to be having fun with the piece, first exploring the scratchy reaches of his instrument, then piling on a more insistent bass that adds dub plunges to the trance.

'Block' (Jenkins)

Without warning, at 8:29, the suite shifts up a gear for this bright, funky chord pattern to which Jenkins adds another written oboe motif and Ratledge the disc's second organ scribble. This isn't to say the piece is a return to the excitement of old – that's simply not possible on *Seven*, an album that sounds as if it was played in the studio on a circle of comfy chairs.

'Down The Road' (Jenkins)

Evoking the ramshackle journeys of the band's van in its sweetly swaying 5/4 rhythm, potholed bass riff, and broken-suspension vibraslap, 'Down The Road' gives Jenkins an amiable platform on which to add a lilting recorder solo before yet another of those massed buzzing oboe themes that are the album's distinctive feature. Babbington then jumps on the bonnet to attack his acoustic bass for the only time on the disc, scrunching and swooping his bow with adorable aplomb while the crazy vehicle bounces through the best cartoon landscape since 'We Did It Again'.

'The German Lesson' (Ratledge)

'Down The Road' fades away after six minutes to leave sunbeam dazzles of synth drone, copiously dipped in the hundreds and thousands of electric piano loops.

'The French Lesson' (Jenkins)

There's no clear division between this and the preceding track. Together, they form just over two minutes of nostalgic summer laze.

The Quintet With Allan Holdsworth

Fusion guitar god Holdsworth was already a rising star when he got the call. He'd played typically elegant and sophisticated lines (including some at blistering speed) on Igginbottom's otherwise dispensable jazz-pop album *Igginbottom's Wrench* (1969). Holdsworth joined Ian Carr in time for *Belladonna*, alongside Roy Babbington and Dave MacRae. You can hear a Carr BBC session of three of the tracks on Nucleus's *Live At The BBC* box (2021), but Holdsworth didn't actually record anything with that band. Instead, he swerved thrillingly sideways to the rock band Tempest (a Colosseum offshoot), enabling him to play alongside drummer Jon Hiseman and help write their excellent 1973 debut album. Holdsworth was clearly equally adept at playing distorted heavy prog and smooth jazz runs.

In November 1973, Soft Machine added him to their quartet. For the band, this solved a problem that had crept in ever since Jenkins decided to sit for the bulk of concerts at second keyboards rather than blow his woodwinds. The two-keyboard-player approach gave depth to the band's intricate lines but rendered the music static and the performance unexciting. They needed a new frontline instrument, and Marshall knew just the man. Holdsworth was certainly the attraction this dour, increasingly impersonal band needed to bring rock fans back into the fold.

The result wasn't just drawing power but a radical reinvention of the band. There would be no gradual transition from format to format as in previous incarnations. To a great extent, Soft Machine started again: a new contract, this time with EMI's prog imprint Harvest (giddy with money after the success of Pink Floyd's *The Dark Side Of The Moon*), a new sound, this time much closer to the prevailing style of smooth, virtuoso fusion, and a new repertoire where they ditched almost everything they'd been playing for new Jenkins compositions.

The band were thus thoroughly rejuvenated. Holdsworth gave them a pinup soloist whose extraordinary technique made jaws drop even within the group. Harvest promised them a sales route into the vast market that had belatedly opened for intricate long-form rock thanks to artists like Yes, Genesis, Mike Oldfield, and King Crimson, who'd all made 1973 prog's breakout year. (Not to mention The Mahavishnu Orchestra, Return To Forever, and Weather Report, who'd done the same for fusion.) Most significantly of all, Soft Machine actually straightened their backs and began to play like they wanted to be there.

I like to think that Holdsworth might have eventually moulded Soft Machine into a vehicle for his work, and that the extraordinary 1980s solo albums for which we chiefly remember him might have happened earlier had he stayed in the band. He managed only two brief compositions on his sole Softs album, *Bundles*, but in later years, surely there would have been more. It wouldn't have mattered if Jenkins had fallen by the wayside, or even if Ratledge eventually slunk away from his stool. Holdsworth wouldn't have drifted so long as he did.

But that wasn't to be. The band was bedevilled by bad finances. A March 1974 tour of the US was abandoned when the funding dried up, and they never returned there. For a guitarist with ambitions, this humiliation must have rung alarm bells. Whether or not it led to open discontent, as early as October 1974, drummer Tony Williams was headhunting Holdsworth, coaxing him to Stockholm to record demos alongside Jack Bruce. These 'lost *Wildlife* sessions' haven't been released officially, but bootlegs exist. Holdsworth had barely settled in and already he was moving out. He stayed in the band for just 17 months – and those, as I've mentioned, were marked by Jenkins's continued dominance of the writing and hence the group's vision – before he suddenly succumbed to the opportunity and absconded to tour America with Williams.

Besides *Bundles*, we have one BBC session and two live releases as our official record of Holdsworth's tenure in the band. The BBC tape, recorded on 10 June 1974, was eventually released on *BBC Radio 1971–1974* and was Soft Machine's last performance for the Corporation. 'Northpoint' is an improvised feature of percussive accents and belchy synths, but the rest are all from the album that was ready for recording the following month: an extended version of Ratledge's chamber piece 'The Man Who Waved At Trains', which gives Holdsworth the chance to call a dramatic, finger-tangling hello, and a 17-minute reading of the bulk of Jenkins's reworked 'Hazard Profile' in which his massive 'Part 1' solo cascades showers of sparks against an energised rock core.

The sessions were imminent when the band played the Montreux Jazz Festival on 4 July, for which occasion a film crew was on hand to document the event. Audio and video of the performance were released as *Switzerland 1974* in 2015. The audience spends the first three and a half minutes of the opener 'Hazard Profile' wondering what the skinny kid with the Gibson is doing on stage. Then he kicks off and even Jenkins – who has seen the feat many times before – seems mesmerised. While Babbington and Marshall react with propulsion, only Ratledge seems superfluous. He's excluded from many shots as if he's no longer part of the new Soft Machine. As if to claim his space, he runs his fingers up and down the now excessively dirty keys in the piece's new closing section. We see Holdsworth nod thanks to the audience afterwards, but he'll learn.

Much of the rest is also from *Bundles*. There's a gorgeous 'The Floating World' in which Marshall comes forward to play glockenspiel while Holdsworth scats the melody hesitantly with a finger in his ear. In 'Bundles' and 'Land Of The Bag Snake' Holdsworth cuts through the rhythm section's barrage, a combination of elegant phrases and breakneck runs, and 'Peff' has Jenkins's sole improvisation, an oboe solo that has a hard time being heard above the onslaught.

Other pieces include the second official rendition of 'Ealing Comedy' (an alarming Babbington improvisation in which he shifts unexpectedly from clean jazz to fuzzed-up lines thickened by Ratledge's Synthi A), 'Joint' (a one-off variant of 'Northpoint'), and a short sequence of material from *Six*. Check out Ratledge, hands in pockets behind his battered gear, staring at Marshall during a long solo on his pristine black kit. The performance ends with 'Penny Hitch' from *Seven*, which Holdsworth claims for his own with yet more coruscating fret work.

On 29 January 1975 – almost a full seven months later – much the same set was recorded for radio live in Bremen, West Germany. This was eventually released as *Floating World Live* (2006). The highlight is an unexpected violin solo by Holdsworth during 'The Man Who Waved At Trains' that makes you wish there were more and – in the Soft Machine way of doing things – presages a time when there *would* be. There's also a new piece destined for *Softs*: Jenkins's elegantly sculpted 'Song Of Aeolus'. But the rendition of 'Hazard Profile' fades out in the middle of Holdsworth's solo, apparently for a commercial break, and Marshall's drum solo is now a Ratledge-wearying ten minutes long.

Bundles (1975)

Personnel:
Roy Babbington: bass
Allan Holdsworth: electric and acoustic guitar
Karl Jenkins: oboe, saxophone, keyboards
John Marshall: drums
Mike Ratledge: keyboards, synthesizer
Ray Warleigh: flute
Recorded July 1974, CBS Studios, London, UK
Producer: Soft Machine
Label: Harvest
Release date: UK: March 1975
Running time: 41:51 (A: 19:57, B: 21:54)

There was no American issue. The 2022 Esoteric Recordings CD packages
Bundles with the Etheridge-era live release *British Tour '75*.

'Hazard Profile Part One' (Jenkins)

Jenkins's most expansive work for the functioning band fills all but the last
minute of side one, though it's not the normal Soft Machine suite. This section,
which alone occupies half the piece's running time (at 9:17), is separated
from the rest by silence. More even than Holdsworth's arrival, the 'Hazard
Profile' construct is an unhelpful litmus test to gauge fan reactions to the new-
look Soft Machine. It's simultaneously a rephrasing of two old compositions
recycled from Jenkins's Nucleus work and evidence of his budding classical
ambitions for the band. It's too acid or it's too alkali. Either way, it's unhelpful
because it just can't be right since Jenkins just can't be right.

'Part One' is certainly dramatic. In the opening 42 seconds, we hear the
slowed, funereal tolling of a cathedral bell and Marshall's threatening military
drum roll, both of which evoke blitz-gutted buildings and scurrying Brits in
useless metal helmets. The piece then pauses for a second's gasp for breath
before erupting into a strolling rhythm made muscular by Holdsworth's
coruscating riff and Babbington's quick-stepping bass. Only Marshall's
dancing accents prevent it sounding like classic-era prog rock. Over the
top, Jenkins layers a disconnected oboe line that climbs repeatedly to heady
peaks. Honestly, if it *is* only the drums that prevent this settling into the
annals of prog's treasures, we've all been robbed.

At 2:50, Holdsworth plays his opening solo, a constantly mutating blaze of
notes that sounds on one hand like an archetypal guitarist's blow and on the
other like a new way to voice Ratledge's organ-playing style. There's certainly
little pause from one run to the next. Ratledge himself provides no more than
fat organ chords to enrich the climaxes. Legend has it that Holdsworth was
never happy with his performance, overdubbing solo after solo after solo,
trying to capture the perfect flight. If only that archive of solos still existed,

and if only we could get to hear it. Imagine a CD-length 'Hazard Profile Part One' with the solos edited consecutively to accommodate them all.

'Hazard Profile Part Two (Toccatina)' (Jenkins)
Following *that* fire could never be easy, and I still can't figure out why Jenkins saddled the rest of the suite with the same title. This first half of this opening is a two-minute piece consisting of solo grand piano in the first half and a delicate chamber duet with acoustic guitar in the second. There's far less interplay than you'd expect, and the two instruments seem to sour each other just when they ought to be poised in mutual rhapsody.

'Hazard Profile Part Three' (Jenkins)
Sinking into Ratledge's organ sound is like nudging your toes into a bed in which a cat has just slept – it's warm, comforting, and makes you feel oddly connected to something living and real. Over this, the band plays a fanfare of prog pomp, with Holdsworth doing his best to phrase each of his lines like Jan Akkerman at his most restrained.

'Hazard Profile Part Four' (Jenkins)
After the 33 seconds of 'Part Three', 'Part Four' settles into that so-significant ambling Pink Floyd tempo for a full-throated guitar riff punctuated by Marshall's cymbals.

'Hazard Profile Part Five' (Jenkins)
This, in turn, lasts 1:26 before the band moves straight into a breakneck 7/8 that kicks and stumbles in support of squelchy unison oboe and synth motifs, with a weird squalling solo by Ratledge, who's audibly delighted by the possibility of his electronics to sound just like someone flailing sideways through a river of fast-flowing lava.

'Gone Sailing' (Holdsworth)
Be careful, CD listeners – 'Gone Sailing' did *not* start side two any more than Steve Hackett's 'Horizons' ended side one of Genesis's *Foxtrot*. This 53-second solo acoustic guitar piece ended side one as if to purposefully deny Jenkins a side-filling suite. It adds a little irrelevant business card for Holdsworth's acoustic guitar abilities to those who might one day need it: some beautifully poised harmonics sandwiching a touch of Steve Howe-style flamenco. It's lovely, but it *could* have started side two if it wanted to be noticed. Then again, who ever noticed 'Horizons'?

'Bundles' (Jenkins)
Side two is a single unbroken suite that at least links to early incarnations of Soft Machine by being an amalgam of pieces by different members of the band – only Babbington doesn't contribute. This three-minute opener begins

with bright, sun-slapped rock, providing another feature for Holdsworth's meaty guitar tone, before veering to a fast, sinewy rhythm over which he rips a series of elegant and busy lead phrases. It culminates in another of those now-familiar climactic climbing fanfares.

'Land Of The Bag Snake' (Holdsworth)
The band drives on with only a shift in rhythm to differentiate this section from 'Bundles'. Here's a swaggering rock swing with monumental chord changes over which Holdsworth continues to solo for another three minutes, now in classic rock style. It's his last solo on the album. Toward the end, the backing subsides to a Pink Floyd vamp, heavy on the Hammond drones.

'The Man Who Waved At Trains' (Ratledge)
The first Ratledge composition shifts pleasingly into Babbington's slinky funk rhythm with pillowy electric piano accents and a dancing melody played in tight unison on soprano sax and electric guitar.

'Peff' (Ratledge)
Ratledge's second section lifts the tempo for three and a half minutes of tricky fusion, eventually with a grinding guitar riff, over which Jenkins solos sweetly and then harshly on reverb-bathed oboe. This ends the rock contingent of the band's rockiest album, though there's still half a side to go.

'Four Gongs Two Drums' (Marshall)
Part of this is the now-obligatory Marshall drum feature – here slops and cascades of toms and wild thrashes at his peripherals. As suggested by the title, the sound is highly restricted, but it's actually the most entertaining Marshall solo to this point.

'The Floating World' (Jenkins)
Those cyclic Terry Riley organ patterns of old return for this long stretch of slinky ambience flavoured with the flute-playing of guest Ray Warleigh. The piece is heavily reminiscent of the Jade Warrior album *Floating World*, which was released – surely coincidentally – the same month Soft Machine recorded *Bundles*.

The Quintets With John Etheridge

Things had seemed back on track until Holdsworth's departure. Instead, from this point until the end of the original band's performing life in December 1978, they fell inexorably apart. In a period lasting less than four years, there were five more line-ups and only one new studio album. The always-woeful finances now became untenable. As fashions in music changed, so the gigs dried up. As creativity slumped, so attention waned, and without attention, there were few opportunities for radio and TV sessions.

The core quartet of Babbington, Jenkins, Marshall, and Ratledge, who'd been together since May 1973, at least seemed stable – that is, until Ratledge quit in January 1976. Infamously, this elevated Soft Machine to the ranks of major groups who'd lost all their original members – a club that, at the time, included Renaissance in 1970 and Fairport Convention in 1971 (though Simon Nicol returned to that band later).

Holdsworth's replacement was John Etheridge, and he was kind enough not only to stick it out to the end (despite then enjoying a much warmer relationship with violinist Stéphane Grappelli), but also to join many of the spinoffs and revivals to follow. Etheridge had past stints in a brace of undistinguished prog rock bands, and membership in Darryl Way's Wolf for its three albums. Though he could certainly play as explosively as Holdsworth (including on the 'Hazard Profile' solo), Etheridge brought a calmer, more introspective guitar sound to the band, which settled well into Jenkins's increasingly formal compositions.

Etheridge was bedded in by the time Soft Machine joined the well-hyped StarTruckin' '75 tour of Europe in August alongside The Mahavishnu Orchestra, Caravan, Wishbone Ash, Renaissance, and others. However, *British Tour '75* (2005), recorded at Nottingham University on 11 October, is the sole official live record of the original Etheridge quintet with Ratledge. The best place to find it currently is the 2022 double-CD *Bundles*. It's mostly the familiar *Bundles* repertoire, but leans towards *Softs* in 'Song Of Aeolus', the delectably weightless 'Out Of Season', and a funky and occasionally boisterous 'Ban-Ban Caliban' that has nothing in common with the earlier 'Neo-Caliban Grides'.

Of the highlights, 'The Man Who Waved At Trains' has some of the old fire, thanks partly to Ratledge's Synthi A belchings that lead straight into his showcase 'JVH'. It sounds horribly dated now, but those sounds were right on the avant-garde cutting-edge in the mid-1970s, even if Ratledge can hardly be credited with handling the sounds with the aplomb of his West German equivalents, let alone the extraordinary ways Pink Floyd found to exploit the technology on the same year's *Wish You Were Here*. The rendition of 'Hazard Profile' also hits the expected peaks, and there's a lengthy jam 'Sign Of Five' as the encore. Depending on how you view such things, the downside may be another ten-minute drum solo.

Etheridge's greatest legacy of the period is *Softs*, recorded at Abbey Road over a somewhat leisurely 14 days in the midst of Ratledge's departure, and including new member Alan Wakeman on saxophone. Wakeman seems more notable for his famous cousin (keyboardist Rick Wakeman) than for his own pedigree, which saw recordings with Graham Collier and composer/pianist Mike Westbrook.

Introducing a sax player into a band that had founded its rebirth on the electric guitar seems bizarre, especially given that Jenkins was capable of playing whatever woodwind lines were required. But both Jenkins and Ratledge were withdrawing from performance, and neither seemed capable any longer of playing the long free-form solos that had once defined the band's live sound. As far as I can tell, the eventual idea was for both Jenkins and Ratledge to become non-playing composers, entrusting the others to carry the band live and in the studio. But this was a route to certain disaster unless the pair considered Soft Machine to merely consist of whatever musicians they brought in for each project. Even then, there would be tension between the classical-music concept of a group of players performing a written score and a rock band free to extrapolate. As we'll see later, they found a different means to achieve the same thing.

The immediate result was a band that moved even further into calculation. Unlike earlier albums, *Softs* was created in the rock way – recording backing tracks using meticulous overdubbing with multiple takes. Only when the rhythm tracks were complete did the soloists fill their allotted spaces over the top, again selecting the best of several passes for each piece just as Holdsworth had done on 'Hazard Profile'. The live show was carefully structured with little collective improvisation and, aside from some token solos, almost no blowing. From this remove it's hard to gauge, but there never seemed to be a Ratledge-sized hole on stage that the others struggled to fill.

Toward the end of the *Softs* sessions – post-Ratledge – Jenkins roped in the others as performers on a side-project album of library music for De Wolfe. It was intended for commercials, incidental TV music, and so on – in retrospect, the shape of things to come for Jenkins. Recordings took place over two days at the company's London studios and involved the four current members of Soft Machine (Babbington, Etheridge, Jenkins, Marshall) plus Jenkins's wife Carol Barratt on piano and Ray Warleigh on flute. Fourteen brief pieces were recorded.

The resulting disc's status as a Soft Machine album is disputable. De Wolfe first released it as *Rubber Riff* in 1976, with the music credited to Jenkins and no performer details. Indeed, it made no sense for potential licensees to know or care who was playing music that was intended to be anonymous. Only in 1994 did a Voiceprint CD reissue slap the name Soft Machine across the front cover for fairly obvious commercial reasons. Further issues have always presented it as a Soft Machine album, though for the purposes of this book, I've chosen to file it in the same category as *Spaced*: music created for extracurricular purposes but not originally intended to be released as by the band.

Certainly, Soft Machine wouldn't have wanted something throwaway like *Rubber Riff* to interfere with the *Softs* sales campaign, and Harvest would have had harsh words to say on the matter. The point of library music is to be safe and generic, for there to be no surprises, no hard edges, no strikingly original tunes – nothing that might make the music unusable as background colour. Indeed, nothing on *Rubber Riff* seems familiar to me today, even if I might have heard it hundreds of times in adverts and TV programs. The very idea that you might *want* to elevate this to a Soft Machine release seems distasteful in the extreme. Moreover, *Rubber Riff* is conceptually troublesome. Successful bands don't need to make library albums. It speaks of failure and desperation. I can't think of *one* that has even come close to enhancing its parent discography – not even the rather good series of discs that Pretty Things made for De Wolfe under the name Electric Banana.

There's little to commend most of the pieces on *Rubber Riff*. The majority of them consist of a simple melody line that is played at the beginning and end of the track – this is the part of the piece that would sell to a client – with a contrasting central section that merely bulks the time. The back cover of the album gives a potted description of each. Hence 'Crunch' is described as 'driving, riffy, dramatic', and 'Pavan' as 'slow, dignified, slightly sad.'

That said, there are some aspects of the disk that *are* worth hearing. Etheridge plays a fine solo in the central section of 'Jombles' ('heavy rock, mid-tempo, guitar'), and 'Rubber Riff' ('busy, fast') contains an interesting synth sound similar to a steel drum. The best track on the disk is 'City Steps' ('bright, neutral, mid-tempo'), whose scurrying, close-packed synths over a tumbling jazz rock riff anticipate Richard Sinclair-period Camel. Even Etheridge's guitar solo has distinct touches of the Andy Latimer to come.

Meanwhile, the churn continued unabated. In July Wakeman quit to work with David Essex (something of a musical crash-landing you'd suppose, though a highly lucrative one), and his replacement Warleigh kept the group afloat only until September when both he and Babbington left.

As well as appearing on *Bundles* and *Rubber Riff*, Warleigh had one of the most prominent resumes of any Softs member. Between our first glimpse of the man decanting himself from Australia in 1960 to play jazz and R&B in the London clubs and his work with Allan Holdsworth in the mid-1970s, Warleigh had become the go-to flautist for a generation of highly regarded British folk artists. You'll find his playing on classic albums by John Renbourn, Bert Jansch, Claire Hamill, Shelagh McDonald, Iain Matthews, and Roy Harper. But Warleigh never forgot the rougher end of Soho either, contributing to John Mayall's *A Hard Road*, Keith Hartley's *The Battle Of North West Six*, and Mike Westbrook's *Metropolis*, among others. Warleigh even made his own album, *Ray Warleigh's First Album* (1969) – but nobody remembers that.

The Warleigh quintet released nothing. Our only record of the line-up is a performance of 'Tale Of Taliesin' filmed for the British TV program *So It Goes* on 7 July, but it's not currently available on YouTube.

To handle a looming European tour, Soft Machine brought in Brand X bassist Percy Jones, with no intention that he would be permanent. Despite his extremely short tenure – just 18 dates, ending at the Newcastle Jazz Festival on 29 October – he also has a resume worth exploring for the sheer quality of the sessions he lucked into. Jones is on Brian Eno's *Another Green World, Before And After Science*, and *Music For Films*, Steve Hackett's *Voyage Of The Acolyte*, Italian band Nova's *Vimana*, Roy Harper's *Bullinamingvase*, and Jack Lancaster's fascinating projects *Peter And The Wolf* (an essential outing narrated by Vivian Stanshall) and *Marscape*.

More radically, Soft Machine replaced Warleigh with electric violinist Ric Sanders, essentially duplicating Holdsworth's violin work with a musician dedicated to the instrument. At the time, Sanders was largely an unknown quantity, having not one session to his name. He was also merely passing through, in his case on the way to The Albion Band, Gordon Giltrap's *The Peacock Party*, and a lifetime gig with Fairport Convention, but he did play Soft Machine's ever-lightening schedule of gigs until the end of their days. The result was a band that – for the first time since the 1969 trio – was all-electric and featured no woodwinds or brass at all.

The sole document of the Jones band is the aforementioned Newcastle Jazz Festival, which was filmed for the BBC. The set has not been released officially, but you can see it on YouTube, complete with a delectable introduction by Spike Milligan. Over 22 minutes, the band run through the *Softs* pieces 'Out Of Season', 'Ban-Ban Caliban' (a feature for the possibilities of Sanders's violin-playing), 'The Tale Of Taliesin', and 'One Over The Eight'. With younger players, less-grizzled hair cut short, *and* a charismatic guitarist, the band appears as a confident fusion combo of the Mahavishnu school. Marshall's kit is now white.

But internally, they were far from confident. They settled on Steve Cook as a permanent replacement for Babbington. Cook was another somewhat untried performer, having coasted for years working for the likes of Pete Atkin, Julie Covington, and Steve Tilston. More encouragingly, he'd played bass on *Psi-Fi* by the Second Hand offshoot Seventh Wave and joined CMU for their second album *Space Cabaret*. As with Sanders, the fact that a band of Soft Machine's pedigree was now recruiting what were essentially novices spoke volumes about the group's finances and prospects.

Any hope of a renaissance on the back of the retrospective *Triple Echo* was lost. The set documented the heights of a different band altogether: more than five sides detailing the remarkable history up to *Six*, and then lip service to the three recent albums, shoved on the very end. That this was a Harvest release – who were essentially denigrating their own product – also spoke volumes.

An increasing lack of money meant that *Alive And Well Recorded In Paris* – their only new album of this period, their last owed to Harvest, and the only official document of these disintegrating years – had to be recorded mostly in concert to save on studio costs. The band pitched up at the Théâtre le Palace for four nights in July 1977 to capture it, but hassles with the recording meant that almost the entire LP came from a single show. Even then, the recording was substandard, requiring repair and enhancement in the studio under the aegis of the band's first outside producer since their debut album.

Though the 2010 CD adds an extra disc with live recordings from the same concert run, in 1977 there was deemed not enough suitable material to fill an entire album, so Jenkins and an uncredited Ratledge added a new studio piece to complete it. The result was eight minutes of disco synths (I'm not kidding) called 'Soft Space'. Harvest thought it might even be a surprise hit like Can's 'I Want More', so they slapped it out on single. The A-side 'Part I (Edited Version)' consisted of the album track's first four minutes. The B-side 'Part II (Edited Disco Version)' faded in on the album track at about 2:44 and played it unaltered through to the end.

The single did what soft things do so embarrassingly: it flopped. The band continued to tour sporadically, including a support slot for a no-doubt-bemused Kevin Ayers, and a reconciliation with Holdsworth for a couple of dates in Portugal. An attempt to reconnect with Wakeman failed. Soft Machine played only one gig in 1978 – the Sound & Musik Festival '78 at Westfalenhalle, Dortmund, West Germany on 8 December – for which Holdsworth stepped in for an Etheridge who was either absent or had moved on. And *that*, silently, finally, was it.

Again.

For now.

Softs (1976)

Personnel:
Roy Babbington: bass
John Etheridge: electric and acoustic guitar
John Marshall: drums
Karl Jenkins: keyboards, synthesizer
Mike Ratledge: synthesizer
Alan Wakeman: saxophones
Recorded January–March 1976, Abbey Road, London, UK
Producer: Soft Machine
Label: Harvest
Release date: UK: June 1976
Running time: 45:23 (A: 23:03, B: 22:20)

There was no American issue. No bonus tracks have ever been released.

'Aubade' (Jenkins)
Since an aubade is a song in praise of dawn, the point of starting with this
glowing, pastoral two-minute singleton (the only one on side one) is surely
to encapsulate still more of the warmth of *Bundles* and settle the listener in
comfortably. As the album's title suggests, *Softs* will not harry or confront:
no buzzsaw edges, no disorienting contrasts, and absolutely no cartoon
chuggery. 'Aubade' stirs only gradually and with the meekest of touches,
punting Alan Wakeman's beautiful soprano sax across the still pool of
Etheridge's acoustic guitar without breaking so much as a ripple.

'The Tale Of Taliesin' (Jenkins)
Karl Jenkins is Welsh, so it's fitting that his most substantial sole-composed
suite, an interweaving of three mythical characters, begins with this evocation
of a Welsh bard whose tales might even have entertained King Arthur. His
grand piano sets down a slightly sour, edgy riff, around which the band
coalesces leisurely, culminating in a gorgeously Etheridge electric guitar solo.
   At 3:05 the piece changes to a whirling sequence of speed-blur riffs
and a contrasting, citrus-sharp Etheridge workout. At 5:15, this in turn, is
pushed aside for a majestic return to the theme now played on guitar and
thickened to within an inch of pompy stodginess by Marshall's gong strokes
and orchestral synth washes that might have been played by an uncredited
Mike Ratledge.

'Ban-Ban Caliban' (Jenkins)
The cinematic fade of 'The Tale Of Taliesin' crosses paths with this more
sinister Ratledge synthscape, with burbling VCS 3 cycles that veer from
channel to channel before themselves being subsumed into a jogger's
workout: all stretched Lycra bouncing back sunlight from sleek, glossy,

constantly shifting curves. Wakeman adds sax lines that are again reminiscent of Jade Warrior, while clattering marimba touches add gazelle-like velocity to Babbington's tarmac-slapping funk.

It's the album's most joyous section, delighting for nine timeless minutes in the climbs and falls of Wakeman's splattery solo and – after another of those bizarre mid-air changes at 12:03 – Etheridge at his hungriest. At 14:19, it returns to the original groove and that massed Jade Warrior winds theme. The section's last-minute piles on the tuned percussion for what sounds surprisingly like Agitation Free's *Malesch*.

'Song Of Aeolus' (Jenkins)
Another crossfade hauls the piano through the synths of Ratledge's official bow-out of the band (though he'll be back, uncredited, on the next disc) and a high-altitude hymn to what is evidently supposed to be the *Odyssey* incarnation of Aeolus. Etheridge is again the featured player, hoisting soaring canopies over the leisurely rock rhythm and Ratledge's cloud-scudded synths.

'Out Of Season' (Jenkins)
Gauged by their silences, there are three separate constructs on side two. The first is an eight-minute pairing of 'Out Of Season' and 'Second Bundle' – again by Jenkins (like the whole of side one), and again elaborated out of his lyrical piano motifs.

Here, almost as if it is a refraction of 'Aubade', the piano flumps against Etheridge's acoustic guitar to suggest a slow-dawning pool where even the midges are too drowsy to swarm. At 1:22, electric guitar and bass enter, shadowing the theme, and Marshall finds subtle things to do with his kit. It's again sumptuous, a high tide mark for fusion at its most tranquil – the kind of moment of sheer delight that adds an aching connection to Mahavishnu Orchestra albums at their fiercest.

'Second Bundle' (Jenkins)
At 5:32, Jenkins lets his last decaying piano note blur into dappled organ touches and sprinkles of synth sunbeams, where it remains for the rest of the piece. A long fade, for once, takes us all the way to silence.

'Kayoo' (Marshall)
Marshall's feature wants to evoke Far Eastern drum patterns, not gamelan but something earthy and Filipino, perhaps, though his style is resolutely western rock. He's given three and a half minutes to indulge the attempt, though on an album this generous it's surely not to fill space.

'The Camden Tandem' (Etheridge, Marshall)
Erupting seamlessly from 'Kayoo', this section adds Etheridge's blistering electric guitar runs to the drum clatter. The idea might have been to emulate

105

the way David Duhig blasted guitar all over Jade Warrior's kecak chanting on *Floating World*. Towards the end, Etheridge seems unable to prevent himself from shifting into melodic phrases to which Marshall concedes a standard rock beat.

'Nexus' (Jenkins)

At 5:29, Jenkins organises a huge chord with virtuoso piano runs and Etheridge's careful phrases. It lasts just 50 seconds.

'One Over The Eight' (Jenkins, Marshall, Etheridge, Wakeman, Babbington)

'Nexus' is about to die away when Marshall again intrudes, establishing a straight funk vehicle for Wakeman's chunky sax bleating. We get exactly four minutes of dance-friendly 4/4 time and head-clearing guitar riff, followed by a long improvised collapse just like the old days and the makings of a new, unrealised groove into the fade.

'Etika' (Etheridge)

The album ends as it began, with a two-minute singleton. But surprisingly, Jenkins hands off to Etheridge for a solo feature on acoustic guitar, likely designed as a response to Holdsworth's 'Gone Sailing' on the previous album.

Alive And Well Recorded In Paris (1978)

Personnel:
Steve Cook: bass
John Etheridge: electric and acoustic guitar
Karl Jenkins: keyboards, synthesizer
John Marshall: drums
Ric Sanders: electric violin
Recorded July 1977 at the Théâtre le Palace, Paris and Advision, London
Producer: Mike Thorne
Label: Harvest
Release date: UK: March 1978
Running time: 38:39 (A: 16:39, B: 22:00)

There was no American issue of this album. The timings given above are for
the original LP, which fades out side one on its applause. On CD, the two
sides are made seamless by the addition of 31 seconds of the band tuning up,
making a total running time of 39:10. 'Soft Space' was released as a single in
1978 (with different edits of the LP version on each side). The 2010 Esoteric
Recordings CD added a disc of live performances (as detailed at the end of
this chapter) along with both sides of the single.

'White Kite' (Jenkins)
At the time, it wasn't unusual for a Soft Machine performance to run together
without break – they'd been doing that since the 1960s. So there's no stretch
in credibility that the first side of this live album is one uninterrupted piece.
However, it's a little curious that it's all written by Jenkins, that it's all new
material, and that the band chose to begin with a fade-in. In reality, *Alive And
Well* is live only as a framework. Yes, many of its basic components were
performed live, but not necessarily in this configuration, and when the music
has been heavily augmented and reshaped in post-production, even the burst
of applause that ends the side (the only element that reveals we're actually on a
stage) must be in doubt. The fade gives us yet another bleary dawn, dewy with
layers of synth patterns that it seems were all played by a very dexterous Jenkins.

'EOS' (Jenkins)
At the end of 'White Kite' a bass throb, a gong roll, and a simple organ riff
escalate tension that is finally released at exactly 3:00 with the arrival of
Marshall's drums, shifting seamlessly into the thundering swing of 'EOS' and
slightly more than a minute of a sculptural Etheridge guitar solo.

'Odds Bullets And Blades, Pt. I' (Jenkins)
This section is a further two minutes of splotchy funk with a reggae guitar riff
and Steve Cook's dub bass. Jenkins is the feature this time, providing a sunny
synth theme that could have come straight out of *Rubber Riff*.

107

'Odds Bullets And Blades, Pt. II' (Jenkins)
At 6:40, Marshall slaps his snare, propelling the band into a frenetic workout over which Etheridge plays elaborate guitar runs.

'Song Of The Sunbird' (Jenkins)
A series of leisurely collapses from 8:45 (over which Etheridge continues to shred as if too hopped-up to read the room) eventually cools the all-too-brief energy sufficiently for this slinky solo synth piece that evokes exactly what the title says: a high glide over fleeces of bubble-topped clouds.

'Puffin' (Jenkins)
Slamming rudely out of the glistening drafts at 10:38, 'Puffin' is a whole different kind of bird. It's a minute of dramatic prog rock chords as a vehicle for Etheridge's squabbling guitar.

'Huffin' (Jenkins)
This is a second section of frantic sandblasting math rock with yet another excellent Etheridge workout. The guitarist seems to find ever more extraordinary ways to deny Ric Sanders an entrance. When Sanders finally makes his first appearance on the disc at 13:52, it's something of a disappointment compared to the wealth of other prog and fusion electric violinists that precede him. His sound is thick, harsh, squalling, but not distinctive, and he's soon divested of things to add except monotonous walls of sawing. Still, this is the noisiest, most exuberant, and least disciplined moment in the entire Soft Machine discography, there's even a glimpse of technical prowess in the scripted lines toward the end, and the crowd loves it.

'Number Three' (Etheridge)
Starting side two, this track is the third such solo acoustic guitar feature on a Soft Machine album, as the title suggests. The listener is first confronted with a curious disconnect. For a long time, it's not at all clear if Etheridge is actually playing the piece or simply tuning up, or whether the flamenco runs and chains of harmonics are scripted or improvised.

'The Nodder' (Jenkins)
At 2:25, the guitar – certainly with the hollow ambience of being live on stage – blurs into Jenkins's plumped-pillow keyboards. The stately 11/8 theme beds a softly shifting rhythm section and a squelchy, synth-enhanced violin theme reminiscent of Gentle Giant's cat impersonations on *Acquiring The Taste*. For long minutes, Etheridge solos on an electric guitar tone as chewy as toffee before slipping sweet and empty back into the mewling theme.

'Surrounding Silence' (Sanders)
This piece shifts pleasingly to four minutes of synth-drone loop and gentle guitar chords over which Sanders plays keening, eastern-inflected violin lines.

'Soft Space' (Jenkins)
The pretence of being a faithful live document is then abandoned. 'Soft Space' jolts the listener into an artificial head environment of interwoven synth pads and dance rhythms – some of them created, no doubt with mischievous glee, by an uncredited Mike Ratledge – over which Jenkins adds another ultra-simple *Rubber Riff* melody. If you're a stickler for band legitimacy, your Soft Machine adventure ends here with these throbbing nightclub beats echoing forever in your skull.

Bonus Disc
So, if *Alive And Well* is a studio-augmented construct, what did Soft Machine *really* sound like in Paris? The 2010 bonus CD adds 46 minutes of unadorned live performance so we can gauge it for ourselves. It includes only one duplicate: a fine take of 'The Nodder' in which Etheridge plays the theme. Notably, most of the pieces are performed standalone, separated by applause.

Much is old. 'Two Down' is a carbon copy of the guitar and drum collision 'The Camden Tandem' on *Softs* – the new name was how it would be presented later in performances by Soft Machine Legacy. There are lovely readings of 'Song Of Aeolus' and 'The Tale Of Taliesin', the latter the only time we hear anything that sounds recognisably like a violin. I'd hesitate to call 'Sideburn' new, as it's just another Marshall drum feature (running the better part of eight minutes), but again, the title was resurrected by the Legacy. 'One Over The Eight' is little more than a generic blow to let off steam at the end of the set.

Of the actual new material, Jenkins's 'K's Riff' consists of a glowering synth motif over the band's knotty rhythms, with a stumbling but workmanlike Etheridge solo, and could easily have been buffed up for the main disc. 'The Spraunce' is hobbled funk, concocted two years earlier by Cook and non-Soft keyboard player Peter Lemer when they were in the Don Rendell Five. And 'Organic Matter' is a two-minute bass solo with enough tricks and diversions to have also been usable in the album proper, though segueing out of it might be tricky.

Ratledge, Jenkins And Further Resurrections

To casual observers, it seemed that Mike Ratledge had dropped off the face of the planet in 1976. This is at least partially true. In the near half-century since, he has contributed to very few albums by others, released only one album under his own name, and never returned to the Soft Machine family on disc or on stage. In 1996, he stopped making music altogether. He has given interviews, but has shown little interest in his performing past. As the last original member who would ever be likely to curate the band's work (something Robert Wyatt certainly could not do), Ratledge's separation bodes ill for a definitive collector's box. Such a box is sure to happen, but it is also sure to suffer from his absence.

Ratledge has said he ceased enjoying being in the band around the time of *Third*. I don't think we can read into that this was caused by a depression like the one that plagued Wyatt, but it's notable that Ratledge's antipathy to the band has never relented, at least not publicly.

He certainly planned a solo career. He composed the score to an obscure 1977 BFI arthouse movie *Riddles Of The Sphinx* – the music would eventually become that sole solo release in 2013. It consists of mesmerising 'Out-Bloody-Rageous'-style synth patterns. He performed some sessions for David Bedford, playing a synth solo on *Instructions For Angels* (1977) and keyboards on 'The Song Of The White Horse', released in 1983. There was a deal with EMI (Harvest's parent corporation), which equipped Ratledge with a home studio. It would likely have involved electronics, like *Softs*, *Riddles Of The Sphinx*, and 'Soft Space'. Computers and sequencers became Ratledge's obsession from then on. But if it was surprising that he never took up CBS's offer of a solo album in 1970 when his writing was prolific, it's not surprising that he never launched himself as a solo act in 1976 when his writing had all but dried up.

And let's wield a little knife and admit that Ratledge wasn't much of a melodicist, either with his themes or when improvising. What he needed was to partner with someone who could provide simple, elegant tunes, and there was the ideal candidate sitting right opposite him.

The easy story – which is actually blindly peddled, even by some fans – is that Karl Jenkins infiltrated Soft Machine, populated it with old mates, and so dominated the writing and the sound with his pedestrian establishment jazz that even Ratledge had enough of him and quit. But whatever tensions might have existed within this tensest of bands, its dissolution can't be blamed on animosity between Ratledge and Jenkins as the two men continued to work closely for decades after. Indeed, they entered their most fruitful musical partnership once the band was over.

There was an attempt to reinvent the pair as electro dance act Planet Earth, releasing an eponymous album in 1978. It consisted mostly of disco versions of classic pieces on cosmic subjects such as Joe Meek's 'Telstar', the *Doctor Who* theme, The Beatles' 'Across The Universe', and (stretching the concept somewhat) the Russian folk song 'Meadowlands'. Another project saw them team up with Ray Warleigh and others under the name Rollercoaster for *Wonderin'*, a 1980 album of Stevie Wonder reinventions. There were also more library albums for De Wolfe, including a series of electronic duets under the name Rubba (as in *Riff*, I assume) promoted as 'progressive electronic keyboards moods with a futuristic sound'. These included *Push Button* (1979), *Movement* (1982), and an album of synth renditions of Christmas carols called *For Christmas, For Children* (1981).

Jenkins tried to revive Soft Machine twice. The first was the 1980 album *Land Of Cockayne*, for which he assembled a cast of Allan Holdsworth, John Marshall, and Ray Warleigh from the band, plus Jack Bruce, Dick Morrissey and others. It's as much a Softs album as anything that follows in this book, so it has its own chapter next, but the project wasn't instigated by the band. Producer Mike Thorne offered Jenkins the opportunity to make one more disc for EMI. Jenkins agreed, but with the proviso that he could use an orchestra. Jenkins and Thorne recorded the album over 13 days in London's Pye Studios and placed the Soft Machine name on the cover.

There was no tour to promote it, but in 1984, Jenkins assembled another iteration of the band to play six nights at Ronnie Scott's, this time adding John Etheridge, John Marshall, and Ray Warleigh from the old band, along with Dave MacRae and Paul Carmichael. The set was mostly *Bundles* and *Softs* material. No recording has been released, and no studio work was undertaken. Ratledge appears not to have participated in either project.

Both ventures were monetary and artistic dead ends. In truth, Jenkins and Ratledge had long since moved on. The De Wolfe albums had gradually eased their focus away from the patently hopeless and corrupt world of rock to the more lucrative world of advertising jingles, which didn't involve all that tawdry touring business. So, the pair went into business together as providers of commercial soundtracks. They quickly found success writing their own music, arranging standards, and recording soundalike versions of famous hits for clients including Audi, BMW, Boots, British Airways, De Beers, Jaguar, Nestlé, Pepsi, Tia Maria, Visa, and Volvo. It was Jenkins and Ratledge who created the music in the famous 'Nicole and Papa' campaign for Renault Clio and the iconic 'Laundrette' spot for Levi Strauss.

In 1994, this work led them to create a dreamy, new age, world-music-flavoured composition called 'Adiemus' for a Delta Air Lines campaign. The public reaction was so positive that Jenkins expanded the piece into a full-blown classical work, *Songs Of Sanctuary* released under the Adiemus name – the ultimate uplift from grubby jazz and rock into the sacrosanct halls of the artistic highbrow. Its success started Jenkins on the path that eventually netted him a knighthood, while Ratledge (who will scarcely get a mention in any discussion of the piece) continues to languish unloved, except by us.

Land Of Cockayne (1981)

Personnel:
Jack Bruce: electric bass
Stu Calver, John Perry, Tony Rivers: vocals
Bill Harman: orchestra leader
Allan Holdsworth, Alan Parker: electric guitar
Karl Jenkins, John Taylor: keyboards, synthesizers
John Marshall: drums
Dick Morrissey: tenor saxophone
Ray Warleigh: alto saxophone, bass flute
Recorded June–July 1980, Pye Studios and Riverside Studios, London, UK
Producer: Mike Thorne
Label: EMI
Release date: UK: March 1981
Running time: 43:52 (A: 22:18, B: 21:34)

There was no American issue of this album. The titles vary in different
territories. No bonus tracks have ever been released.

'Over 'N' Above' (Jenkins)

Land Of Cockayne is an aberrant work for more than just the obvious
reasons. It is the band's only concept album, and the only one of the official
original run not to have track segue. Of the ten pieces, only four are fused
into pairs, and those are joined only because the second track begins while
the previous one is fading. All the others are separated by silences, possibly
a calculation to increase the likelihood of radio play. Essentially, it's a big-
budget *Rubber Riff*, complete with a large *ad hoc* string section and a trio of
singers.

The concept itself is hazy and – given that there are no lyrics – suggested
merely by the song titles and liner notes. Here, Jenkins (who already gave
us pieces about Taliesin, Caliban, and Aeolus) digs again into European
mythology to describe the topsy-turvy utopia of Cockaigne, a place
where long-suffering peasants are promised their just desserts: heaven for
simpletons. With straight face, and surely well aware that today the title is
going to be read as 'cocaine', the notes precis the medieval poems, listing
a bunch of fantasies visitors can enjoy in the place, including 'naked nuns
[who] bathe in rivers of sweet milk'.

There's at least a strong Soft Machine contingent among the session players.
Aside from Jenkins himself, Holdsworth, Marshall, and Warleigh were roped
in. But the point, just like *Rubber Riff*, was to play Jenkins's music faithfully
and facelessly.

'Over 'N' Above' smashes the listener straight into a leisurely soft rock
rhythm that sounds like a cross between The Alan Parsons Project and
ABBA's 'Eagle'. But just when you think it ought to fly, Jenkins inserts a sax

melody that evokes the more dispensable of his library music and drops the thing flat. The vocal harmonies, sumptuous string sweeps, and chunky 'Baker Street' sax drench the rest in a curdled, desperate-sounding AOR that is maintained for more than seven wearying minutes.

'Lotus Groves' (Jenkins)
Assuming 'Over 'N' Above' was meant as an overture, 'Lotus Groves' is our first peek into Cockayne. A promising ethnic opening is soon flittered away for five minutes of jaunty synth sounds, genteel flute accents, and a nursery rhyme melody.

'Isle Of The Blessed' (Jenkins)
Opening the first of the two pairs, 'Isle Of The Blessed' sets up sumptuous Electric Light Orchestra-style strings and then – just where that band would launch into rock'n'roll – keeps circling it around and around.

'Panoramania' (Jenkins)
There's much more of the classic Jenkins-era Soft Machine sound here, though filtered through the *Rubber Riff* sensibility. At least the rhythm has glimpses of funk and fusion, and when the sax isn't drowned in strings it has a pleasing abrasion. But a long electric piano solo pads it out, and Jack Bruce – the man who gave us that enthralling bass muscle on Frank Zappa's 'Apostrophe'', out-Hoppering Hopper on the fuzz – here just slaps a few accents from time to time.

'Behind The Crystal Curtain' (Jenkins)
Side one ends with slightly under a minute of astringent synths and indecently undressed sax.

'Palace Of Glass' (Jenkins)
The second pair is, at 11 minutes, the album's longest uninterrupted stretch of music. It begins with an atmospheric fade into a moment of visceral drama that is then tossed aside for more of that 'Lotus Groves' blend of cyclical synths and lulling bass flute. Admittedly, it's beautiful, especially when it holds a single unwavering chord for 50 seconds, including placidly sailing through an abrupt John Marshall drum storm at the end.

'Hot-Biscuit Slim' (Jenkins)
This bright, fat-synth funk comes across like an amalgam of the standard American disco and fusion traits of the late 1970s – we're certainly not in the realm of what was happening in British music at the time. An attractive sax theme and Bruce's most assertive bass playing add welcome punch. But we've heard this groove before, and yet more lengthy sax and Rhodes solos fail to lift the piece.

'(Black) Velvet Mountain' (Jenkins)

Synth pads and soft strings skid into five minutes of swoony rock rhythm and bronzed, sunset-like chords. Allan Holdsworth gets his first feature of the disc, though it's only to enunciate Jenkins's repetitive line. Instead, the sax again gets the solo, and once more in that treacle-thick 'Baker Street' style.

'Sly Monkey' (Jenkins)

This is another five minutes of alternating stop/start funk and swooning sax lines, though Bruce seems bored enough to be mischievous, and Holdsworth at last gets the chance to blow.

'"A Lot Of What You Fancy....."' (Jenkins)

Jenkins's final piece for the band is an uncontentious 35 seconds of bland *Rubber Riff*-style acoustic piano and sax.

Spinoffs And Revivals

Up until this point, this book has focused on a clear central core: a single band that for much of its career was a full-time operation even if – as with Robert Wyatt in 1970 and Elton Dean in 1971 – some members engaged in side projects during the band's downtime. But almost everything that follows was a part-time occupation, sometimes no more than a small collection of musicians coming together for a recording session, a string of dates, the makings of a tour, or promotional activities. Those musicians interacted with others in a cat's cradle of connections, forming a plethora of temporary or *ad hoc* groupings. Even the most prominent of the bands that resulted were in a continual state of flux as players shuffled projects and priorities.

A complete exploration of this scene would fill hundreds of pages and produce a Gordian knot of players that makes Pete Frame's Soft Machine family tree look like the smallest of twigs. To give one example, Hugh Hopper was a member of Soft Heap, Soft Head, Soft Ware, Polysoft, Soft Works, Soft Mountain, Soft Bounds, and Soft Machine Legacy. He recorded – often with similar personnel – as Hopper/Gowen, Hopper/Gowen/Morris, Hopper/Sinclair, Hopper Goes Dutch, The Hugh Hopper Band, Hopper/ Kramer, Hopper/Hewins, Hopper/Hewins/Pyle, Hopper/Tate, and many more. He contributed to albums in a similar style by bands like Gilgamesh, Mother Gong, Pip Pyle's Equipe Out, In Cahoots, Short Wave, Conglomerate, Caveman Shoestore, Gizmo, Brainville, Caravan, Glass Cage, and Clear Frame. There are also a bunch of solo releases. Elton Dean's curriculum is just as rich and confusing, and often collides with Hopper's. Even a project with the highest profile was usually simply that: a project. Other projects were interwoven to the ends of the players' days.

The reality of being a prog rock, jazz fusion, or Canterbury Scene performer in the late 1970s and beyond meant it's no surprise there was so much fragmentation that only a handful of the luckier projects achieved anything like longevity or that many players teetered on the edge of following their muse fruitlessly, dropping into more-commercial work merely to make a living, or gave up altogether. It was extremely hard to gain media attention. The radio conduit had all but dried up. Audiences were small, sales were meagre, and touring was likely to be financially ruinous. Your internal differences were set against external indifference. The glory years were most definitely over and never seemed to be coming back, and you had to somehow retain the fans you had. You'd probably never again command an advance or have a worthwhile recording budget. It was going to become difficult to even replace broken equipment, and everything you did was an economic compromise. Friendly venues were oases in far-flung European scenes that largely made many British players exiles from their homeland. And moreover, you had to balance *all this* against your personal life and home pressures.

A few band names at least came with stature to carry them forward. As prog rock has revived over the past two decades, heritage bands from its golden age have become one of its biggest draws. The musicians, many of them now comfortable enough in their middle age to regard music-making as hobby, creative outlet, and a little reminder of the fire of their youth, find themselves back in demand.

In the 1970s, their status as honorary head of the Canterbury Scene notwithstanding, Soft Machine had generally sourced new members from outside that Scene. This isn't surprising given that the band's sound became so far removed from the template we associate with Caravan and Hatfield And The North and headed instead into Nucleus-style virtuoso fusion.

Posthumously, however, the opposite happened. Since Soft Machine had been such a revered figurehead for the style, the later bands that evoked its name often drew from the Scene alumni, using the 'Soft' in the band name to signify a certain kind of music for a certain audience. Both 'Canterbury Scene' and 'Soft Machine' still have cachet, it's the earlier work that is best remembered, and though nothing that follows in this book ever hit the commercial heights of *Third* (nor was anyone under any misapprehension that it could), the revivals have attracted bookings, record contracts, and fans.

But with the status comes a conservative attitude toward the music. The Canterbury Scene has ossified into a recognisable style. Whether you're a heritage band or a new group, the 'Canterbury Scene' tag is your indicator, and you play within that limit. Recent Softs revivals have been a mixture of early-era highlights and new pieces, balanced carefully to match the audience's tolerance of unfamiliar work. New studio albums don't stray too far from the 1970s template. Bands on the Soft Machine tier don't have the commercial leeway to be as radical as, say, King Crimson. So the gigs and releases are an ever-spinning refraction of past facets – often incredibly good, always pleasingly adept, but not pushing the envelope to any dangerous degree.

What follows picks its way through the 'Soft' studio releases like stepping stones through quicksand. For each of these albums, there are many others that don't have the appellation and, hence, don't get an entry. It's arbitrary and superficial, I know, but there's no other way to meaningfully navigate the 37 years from the Soft Machine of *Land Of Cockayne* to that of *Hidden Details* and *Other Doors*. Since we need them both, we need the stepping stones between: hence this complex and selective adjunct to the book.

The entries are chronological, so that means we have to begin by moving backwards in time a bit.

Soft Heap And Soft Head

For Elton Dean and Hugh Hopper, the parent band never went away. Both returned to the Softs family in 1978, and both died as members of Soft Machine Legacy. In effect, the trajectory given in this chapter is the one that prevailed – a continuity into the present – whereas the Jenkins version of Soft Machine is the aberration.

Like Wyatt, Dean and Hopper both took advantage of the CBS deal to record a solo album. Dean's eponymous 1971 album (later renamed *Just Us* on CD) saw him employ a familiar cast on pieces that blurred into the parent style and repertoire, including a studio version of 'Neo-Caliban Grides'. Unsurprisingly, given Phil Howard's participation, it is more of the frantic free-blowing that Howard brought to the Softs. If you like side one of *Fifth,* you'll surely like this just as much.

The same year, Dean joined the Centipede project and began session work with artists across the rock and blues spectrum, including Heads Hands & Feet, Mike Hugg, Reg King, and Alexis Korner. He played with Chris Mcgregor's Brotherhood Of Breath alongside Mark Charig, Nick Evans, and Mongezi Feza, among many others, joined Feza to back his Assagai colleague Dudu Pukawa on *Diamond Express*, and played with the usual suspects on Julie Tippetts's *Sunset Glow*, Carla Bley's *European Tour 1977*, and Keith Tippett's Ark's *Frames*.

Dean also led bands of his own. The first album prompted the short-lived free jazz unit Just Us, which recorded nothing more. In 1975, he created Elton Dean's Ninesense, a nine-piece consisting of a Soft Machine-style rhythm section of keyboards (in this case Keith Tippett), bass, and drums and a crowded brass and woodwind section involving Charig (and briefly Feza) among others. They managed one studio album – *Happy Daze* (1977) – but you can hear them collide at their big band best in performance on *Oh! For The Edge* (1976) and the retrospective *Live At The BBC* (2003). As you'd expect, the key here is the Soft Machine septet.

In 1977 alone, Dean also released *They All Be On This Old Road* credited to The Elton Dean Quartet (including Tippett on piano), the Alan Skidmore collaboration *El Skid*, and *The Cheque Is In The Mail* as a trio with Kenny Wheeler and Joe Gallivan.

While Dean blew gusts and gales, Hopper turned to tapes. His CBS album was *1984*, recorded quickly between Soft Machine tours in July and August 1972. Mixing flurries of jazz fusion with wheezing loops and tape manipulations, it set up the sound world and ideas for '1983' on *Six*, recorded three months later. Thematically related to George Orwell's *Nineteen Eighty-Four* – if only by its brooding, unsettled music – the album consists of two lengthy tracks and a bundle of interludes. 'Miniluv', the first of the epics, places disconcerting trumpet fanfares over an urban wasteland of electric bass and disconnected percussion, sitting somewhere between the clatter of Frank Zappa's midnight train on The Mothers of Invention's 'The Chrome-

Plated Megaphone Of Destiny' (a certain influence: Hopper declared himself a Zappa fan) and the industrial clang of the embryonic West German kosmische bands. Toward the end, it erupts into terrifying psychedelic loops that refuse to focus into voices.

'Minipax I' is jaunty but grim big-band jazz rock much like the swagger of Carla Bley's monumental *Escalator Over The Hill*, again scarified by spectral voices that command, weep, and scream. It's played by an extraordinary roll call of colleagues, including Lol Coxhill, Nick Evans, Pye Hastings, John Marshall, and Gary Windo. Most of these also add to 'Minipax II', loops of brassy declamations over manipulated free squall, much of it backwards, and 'Minitrue', a brief return to Bley's cheerless Teutonic drinking dens. The second epic, 'Miniplenty', is a grim loop collage that also escalates into distorted bass scrunches and cymbal strikes like pain shrill, then darkens to 'Minitrue Reprise', a requiem of wounded bird cries on saxophone.

The 1998 CD issue adds 'Miniluv Reprise', which actually sounds more like a blowing version of 'Minipax I' with the same Bierkeller band. Its dominant feature is hollow slabs of Hastings's electric guitar. Subsequent releases have added a host more bonus tracks, rounding out further one of the best and most radical of the Soft Machine family of works.

Following his departure from the parent group in May 1973, Hopper teamed with percussionist Stomu Yamash'ta for *Freedom Is Frightening* and *One By One*, joined fusion group Isotope for *Illusion* and *Deep End*, and played alongside Robert Wyatt – on sessions for Gary Windo later released on *His Master's Bones* (1996) – and Dean on Carla Bley's *European Tour 1977*.

The key release of the period was the fat, fuzzy, and savagely entertaining second solo album *Hopper Tunity Box* (1977), whose contributors included Dean, Charig, Windo, and Dave Stewart. Its title references a *Nineteen Eighty-Four* dystopia of a different kind: the British TV talent show *Opportunity Knocks* hosted by Stalin-esque namesake Hughie Green. Roy Harper had spat out Green's insincere catchphrase 'and I mean that most sincerely' on Pink Floyd's 'Have A Cigar' in 1975. Highlights include Hopper's sped-up fuzz bass on a new version of 'Miniluv', Stewart's squonking organ solos on 'Gnat Prong', the lilting tape play on 'The Lonely Sea And The Sky', and the monstrous tangle of loops and electronics that enfold 'Mobile Mobile'. Best of all is the calming and delightful album closer 'Oyster Perpetual', an interplay of Hopper's multitracked bass. It's another essential album and one that could have credited Soft Machine at their peak.

As early as Hopper's *Monster Band*, recorded in 1973 and 1974 but not released until 1978, Dean and Hopper had begun circling each other, heading toward an ever-tighter collaboration on *Cruel But Fair* (1977) and *Mercy Dash* (recorded in 1977), both also featuring Keith Tippett and Joe Gallivan. In 1978, Dean teamed up with keyboard player Alan Gowen and drummer Pip Pyle for informal blowing sessions in Gowen's front room and invited Hopper to join in. Immediately realizing the quartet's potential, they chose a moniker signifying half of Soft Machine and arranged 'Heap' from the first letters of their given names.

Gowen and Pyle had particularly rich pedigrees in the scene, and here we dive into just a hitch or two of that Gordian knot I mentioned in the previous chapter. Gowen had led Gilgamesh, whose eponymous first album in 1975 is one of the treasures of the wider Canterbury Scene firmament. Besides a stint in Gong and romantic entanglements with two of Robert Wyatt's partners, Pyle was instrumental in the creation of another Canterbury Scene highlight, Hatfield And The North, alongside Dave Stewart (of Egg and Khan), Phil Miller (of Caravan and Matching Mole), and our old Wilde Flowers friend and Caravan stalwart Richard Sinclair. Pyle played on Hatfield's eponymous 1974 debut and *The Rotters' Club* (1975). He also wrote one of their loveliest pieces – 'Fitter Stoke Has A Bath' – which the band recorded twice and which is the second song in this book to name-check Wyatt's wife Pam (after 'Why Am I So Short?'). More live and studio recordings from the period are available officially on *Hatwise Choice* (2005) and *Hattitude* (2006), though the unofficial releases *Live '74* (2019) and *Live 1973* (2020) might be easier to find.

In 1975, Gowen and Stewart formed a side project, National Health, with Miller, Bill Bruford, and Gilgamesh bassist Neil Murray. When both Gilgamesh and Hatfield And The North fell apart and Bruford quit, the others brought in Pyle, only for all-too-familiar creative differences between Stewart and the others – Stewart was only interested in playing structured music, they favoured improvisation – to collapse the band. Gowen himself quit in March 1977 after recording their eponymous album (released in February 1978). Murray eventually let the team down by slumming it to worldwide adulation in Whitesnake.

A reorganised National Health consisting of Stewart, Miller, Pyle, and bassist John Greaves toured Europe in the spring of 1978 on the back of the LP. Greaves also had an excellent pedigree, having played in Henry Cow (on *Legend, Unrest, In Praise Of Learning*, and *Concerts*) and released the 1977 album *Kew.Rhone* with Peter Blegvad of Slapp Happy.

Unfortunately, when it came to Soft Heap touring in May, Pyle's obligation to National Health took precedence. Dean, Hopper, and Gowen drafted in the all but unknown Dave Sheen to deputise – his only previous notable release was the eponymous 1971 album by jazz rock band Ben. This shifted the 'Heap' to 'Head' for their earliest release, the live album *Rogue Element* captured at Jackie Barbier's club À L'Ouest de la Grosne in Bresse-Sur-Grosne, France. The LP was credited to the four men separately, though the Soft Head name appeared on the back cover.

In Dean's blustery 'Seven For Lee', Hopper prods moments of swing into the 7/8 rhythm. Hopper's only written contribution here, 'Seven Drones' is nothing to do with the Daevid Allen album of that title. It's actually freeform and chaotic, moving straight into Gowen's 'Remain So', a jigsaw puzzle of riffs and prickly solos. Gowen's 'C.R.R.C.' slinks catlike down its French backstreets, with Dean blowing every sultry café cliché he can think of. Dean's own 'One Three Nine' ends the set in a rollicking jazz counterpoint.

Freed from the gravity and scrutiny of a Soft Machine release, where every note must be measured because it's important, *Rogue Element* shows four fine players having a great deal of fun with their onstage invention. Happily, it will be the template for all the attitude to follow.

The album is now best heard in the expanded 1996 CD edition, which added Dean's massive 'Ranova', in which Hopper dribbles basketball bass through a wall of dissonant defenders, and Gowen's stop/start 'C You Again' (which is better than the title suggests).

In the summer, the reformed National Health recorded *Of Queues And Cures*, and Gowen revived the Gilgamesh name for the second and final album *Another Fine Tune You've Got Me Into* (1978), a studio-only project that integrated Hopper into the sound. National Health then attempted to absorb ex-Henry Cow bassoonist Lindsay Cooper and cellist Georgie Born, and it was during gaps in these rehearsals in October that the original Soft Heap quartet finally recorded the group's sole studio album (see the following chapter). But Stewart walked from National Health, apparently for the same reason as before: the others wanted to improvise and he didn't. But the story makes little sense, as both Cooper and Born required written parts so there should have been *more* structure rather than less. It likely masked a greater problem. The band's inability to find a keyboard player to replace Stewart testifies damningly to National Health's prospects and status. Stewart's reaction to another decade of poverty was to hitch himself to Bruford, and eventually to dive into commercial pop, which netted him a (still) mind-blowing UK four week number one hit single in 1981.

But wait – things get complicated now. Soft Heap, in their original form, seem to have played only two gigs. The first was at London's Phoenix Club on 22 November 1978. This was recorded and eventually released as *Al Dente* in 2008. It includes performances of 'Fara' and 'Circle Line' from the *Soft Heap* album, Gowen's restless, jumpy 'Sleeping House' – a platform for Dean's frantic saxello blasts and Gowen's cascading electric piano runs – and edgy versions of 'Remain So' and 'C.R.R.C.' where Pyle adds wintry flurries to the urban back streets. The album ends with a jagged 'Seven For Lee' in which Gowen strains for his electric piano to be heard over Pyle's end-of-set exuberance. Gowen soon gives up and joins Dean and Hopper in freeform mayhem.

The second gig was at London's 100 Club on 4 December. Sadly, there would be no more, as Hopper now bowed out. On his own admission, he didn't play bass again for more than a year. Meanwhile, National Health had ditched Cooper and Born, and focused on the core of Miller, Pyle, and Greaves. They tried to bring in Art Zoyd guitarist Alain Eckert, but when this failed National Health fell into hiatus. Greaves was then able to take Hopper's slot in Soft Heap in January 1979. But subsequently, Gowen revived National Health with Pyle and Greaves, and for most of 1979, all three were engaged playing extensive but penniless tours of Europe and the US, putting Soft Heap back on hold. In December, Gowen, Greaves, and Pyle reunited with Dean for a short Soft Heap UK tour sponsored by the Jazz Centre Society, which at least netted them some fees.

National Health regrouped in 1980, but Gowen had a recurring illness that became terminal. He succumbed to leukaemia in 1981 at the age of just 33.

The quartet of Dean, Pyle, Greaves, and guitarist Mark Hewins (augmented by Eckert) recorded a second Soft Heap live set at Jackie Barbier's club in March 1982. It was released in 1995 as *A Veritable Centaur,* along with the lengthy studio track 'Toot De Sweet' recorded for the BBC in 1983.

From the start, *A Veritable Centaur* is a beast of a different spoke. It's a Gong-style collage of live pieces that may well have been altered beyond recognition at some point in post-production. That's not a criticism as such, as the results are absolutely phenomenal. The opener 'Dying Dolphins' is two minutes of electronic swoops and squiggles, possibly recorded in a studio. On the title track, Greaves recites a poem over more electronic squeals and some frenetic free jazz from Dean and Pyle, recalling Daevid Allen's early performance work.

'Space Funk' is *not* a De Wolfe reject, though it sounds like one in the opening seconds – that is, before Dean and Hewins deconstruct the melody with a monstrous psychedelic maelstrom that continues unabated through forests of disembowelled squirrels in 'Tunnel Vision' and (wait for it) 'Nutty Dread' (which is a pretty funny title under the circumstances).

'Bossa Nochance' seems to have nothing in common with its namesake, the delectable Richard Sinclair spot on *Hatfield And The North,* but consists of hallucinogenic Indian motifs above which Dean's mischievous snake shows an occasional mesmeric hood before settling into what I swear is an impersonation of Gong member Didier Malherbe. 'Jackie's Acrylic Coat' also seems to channel trilogy-era Gong: disconnected dub over which words unspool in slippery clutches. Wait a few more years and you'd mistake this for an Ozric Tentacles offshoot.

The dub continues in 'Thaid Up', which wants to be comprehensible free jazz but rapidly disintegrates in oceans of reverb, and 'A Flap', which sees Pyle abandon his reggae pretensions once Dean takes flight. Finally, Greaves stomps on his fuzz box for the demonic intrusion of 'Day The Thirst Stood Still', a punishment of trippy riches. The bonus track 'Toot De Sweet' is an identical-format free blow running a brain-mashing 26 minutes.

That was it for Soft Heap. National Health – with a core line-up of Pyle, Greaves, Stewart, and Miller – released their third and final studio album *D.S. Al Coda,* in 1982, consisting entirely of Gowen pieces recorded in his memory. There was a retrospective release *Playtime* (2001), assembled from two 1979 concerts. Readers are also pointed toward the retrospective *Missing Pieces* (1996), which mops up early work by the band, the collection of Gilgamesh rarities *Arriving Twice* (2000), which similarly includes early work with future Soft Machine member Steve Cook, the eerie 1980 Gowen/Hopper album *Two Rainbows Daily*, and the 1982 Gowen/Miller/Sinclair/Tomkins album *Before A Word Is Said*. But all that – to coin a Gong phrase – is only the beginning of the story.

Subsequently, Pyle continued to wind his way through Equipe Out, Gong (for the 1992 Daevid Allen reunion album *Shapeshifter*), Short Wave, Brainville, In Cahoots, and many more. He died in 2006.

The tangled tale of Gilgamesh, Hatfield And The North, National Health, and Soft Heap is typical of the tumbling decline of those years. The bands are well remembered and left a fine legacy. But they hardly survived in the moment, pushing against intractable obstacles and daunting odds. Whereas Soft Machine had gained enough gravity to continue recording (including that Jenkins indulgence *Land Of Cockayne*), these bands largely could not. Given the constant dance of personnel and fortunes, there are gaps in their histories, places where the bands blur to silence. We don't have a comprehensive picture of any of them, and there will almost certainly never be a bedrock big enough to make a proper multi-disc documentation commercially viable, however much we might long to see it and hence know that all these people and all this music actually meant something.

Soft Heap (1978)

Personnel:
Mark Charig: trumpet
Elton Dean: saxophones
Alan Gowen: keyboards, synthesizer
Hugh Hopper: bass
Radu Malfatti: trombone
Pip Pyle: drums
Recorded October 1978, Pathway Studios, London, UK
Producer: Soft Heap
Label: Charly
Release date: UK: 1979
Running time: 42:37 (A: 22:41, B: 19:56)

The vinyl version was only issued in the UK in 1979 and Japan in 1982. No
bonus tracks have ever been released.

'Circle Line' (Hopper)

This outstanding opener hardly evokes the dirty, crowded train route
the players used in order to meet up, though it does have some of its
interminable delays. Slow to the point of an aching stasis, the introduction's
soft harmonic bass lulls you into a receptive space where Dean's sinuous sax,
Gowen's slippery glides of organ notes, and Pyle's gentle kit kisses move
in mesmerising spirals. Only at 3:44 does the piece accumulate a clattering
busyness, but this subsides a minute later.

The rest is a band improvising on the brink of dreams, crafting monuments
from barely enunciated thoughts and moments of bliss from glancing chance
encounters.

'A.W.O.L.' (Gowen, Pyle, Dean)

The most substantial of side one's three tracks, 'A.W.O.L.', has a frenetic
urgency as it squirms around Dean's free-jazz bleats, Pyle's restless
propulsions and Gowen's otherworldly synth gloop. Eventually, powerful
riffs organise themselves only to erupt into harrowing stumbles and bulky
collapses. Gowen's glowering, glass-eyed synth solo toward the end is
magnificent, which makes the decision to fade out the track a real shame. To
fall apart in disarray is what this masterpiece required.

'Petit 3's' (Gowen)

A six-minute stretch of smoky late-night jazz, the piece is a vehicle for
Dean's saxophone playing at its most aching and joyless. Gowen counters
with glimmers of warm organ but cannot lift the piece out of its melancholy.
The title refers to a sluggish rhythm that surges aimlessly and goes
nowhere.

123

'Terra Nova' (Dean)

Home – at least Hopper's home, as given in the title – begins with a long slow-motion unison for bass and sax that sags repeatedly as if each player is trying to pull the other back. The album's first conventional rhythm arrives at 2:53, though it's a painfully disjointed one, with bass and drums pushing weird funk shapes hard into each other until they fuse momentarily then snap back apart. Dean's solo is all jabs and retreats. The rhythm breaks down for good at 8:14, but there are another two minutes in which the bass and sax finally manage to bring each other to a standstill.

'Fara' (Dean)

For this track alone, the core band is joined by trumpeter Mark Charig and trombonist Radu Malfatti. They take the lead from the start, winding exhausted lines over a slow and listless backing. Dean plays slack notes in counterpoint.

'Short Hand' (Gowen)

This short closer is the album's most conventional piece. It's a drum and sax duet bookended by jumpy jazz that scuttles unpredictably across the staves, pausing repeatedly before leaping off again in whatever direction seems to be the most alarming.

Soft Ware, Soft Works, Soft Mountain And Soft Bounds

Though many of the players remained active in the lean years that followed, there was no new 'Soft' studio release for more than 20 years. For the prog rock generation of musicians that hadn't ascended to superstardom, the 1980s and 1990s were challenging – not just because the industry was no longer interested, but because these decades coincided with the time they needed to stabilise their home lives, raise families, and secure a regular income. This led many to shelve the musical pretensions altogether or regard them merely as a hobby. Hopper and Dean turned 40 in 1985, and for a while, both gave up music.

Jazz's leap onto the rock bandwagon in the late 1960s didn't seem like such a good move now that jazz had been so thoroughly subsumed by fusion and fusion was, in turn, out of favour. A few clubs still held blowing sessions, but the jazz scene was essentially dead for all but the smooth swingers and traditionalists, a handful of virtuosos, and those willing to nail themselves to the latest fashion in dance music and street pop.

But a remarkable thing happened in the late 1990s. People started listening to the old music again, playing it, broadcasting it, and buying it in big enough numbers to spark a renaissance. Whether it was because contemporary music seemed worn out, those who'd persistently bleated the punk gospel were themselves now old and devalued, or the kids of the 1970s experienced the inevitable 20-year nostalgia kick, but the music of rock and fusion's golden age suddenly made sense again. The result was the flood of new archival releases by Soft Machine (as detailed in this book) – extraordinary concerts that had seemed lost to time – and labels such as Voiceprint and MoonJune that actively wanted to release new music by the Canterbury Scene players in the same way that Virgin had wanted to sign and disseminate the Softs family in the early 1970s.

By the time the Soft Machine name was revived, prog rock's rehabilitation was well underway. Hopper and Dean simply reacted logically, signifying their music to audiences that would be turned on by the Soft Machine association – not least because of Wyatt's fame and stature – but didn't give a hoot about all the music the men had made in the meantime.

Of that unaffiliated music, the most accessible was by Hugh Hopper, who revived not only his interest in rock but also in the experiments that had characterised *Third* and *1984*.

Hooligan Romantics (1994) saw him add samples to a bed of mostly live recordings from clubs in Holland and France, and in a punishing version of 'Miniluv' pit Dean's blasts against a rush of heavy guitar rock. *A Remark Hugh Made* – a collaboration with Kramer the same year – quested outward in all directions, including bright, poppy trances unsettled by Gary Windo's scarified sax (such as 'A Streetcar Named Desire' and 'John Milton Is Dead') and coruscating fractals of psychedelia in 'The Twelve Chairs'. But the British music scene was fixated on emerging Britpop and didn't listen.

Hopper worked with Richard Sinclair (on the lovely joint album *Somewhere In France*), Wyatt, and Daevid Allen, and added bass on a version of Caravan's 'Ride' for their 2000 reinvention of old songs *All Over You...Too*. A 1996 compilation of Hopper's solo work was titled *Best Soft*, a double meaning that might have had little justification but did stake a claim for him being more than just the overlooked later member who used to drive the van. Making that claim was necessary, too, given that the same year's CD issue of the frantic free jazz album *Mercy Dash* (by Hopper, Dean, Tippett, and Joe Gallivan) came with a large notice on the front: 'Played in Soft Machine'. Get past that, and the track 'Brass Wind Bells' shows a band a hundred paces further out than the Softs *ever* dared venture.

But Hopper's finest solo release was *Jazzloops* (2002) – a return to the congested soundscapes of *1984* – in which snippets of Dean, Wyatt, John Marshall, Didier Malherbe, and many others fight for airspace against Hopper's encroaching thickets of tape noise.

Much more Hopper music was released after his death in the ten-volume series *Dedicated To Hugh* released by Gonzo Multimedia in 2014 and 2015.

In 1998, while his solo work was progressing, Hopper joined French jazz band Collectif Polysons to perform Soft Machine classics under the joint name Polysoft. With Dean sitting in and Emmanuel Bex providing the Ratledge role, they immortalised the set live in September 2002 at Le Triton, a small club (seating less than 200 people) in Paris with which we will become very familiar. *Tribute To Soft Machine* (2003) came in a cover that directly referenced *Third*. Though that album was of course featured heavily – an updated 'Facelift' reinvented as chamber and computer chaos, a slinky, alluring 'Slightly All The Time', a triumphant run through the 'Noisette'/'Backwards' sequence – there were also exuberant renditions of 'Pig' and an all-sax instrumental 'Dedicated To You, But You Weren't Listening' from *Volume Two*, and punchy updates of 'Kings And Queens' from *Fourth*, 'As If' from *Fifth*, and 'Gesolreut' and 'Chloe And The Pirates' from *Six*. In other words, the perfect Hopper-era primer.

The Polysoft adventure triggered revivals of the Soft Machine sound using a core of Hopper and Dean with whatever other alumni and associated personnel could be coaxed into joining. The first aggregation Soft Ware (or SoftWare, or even SoftWhere) added Marshall and Keith Tippett for a September 1999 gig in Augustusburg, Germany but failed to make it into a studio or memorialise their set on an official recording.

Soft Ware seemed to rely mostly on new material. The same was true of the second revival Soft Works, which replaced Tippett with Allan Holdsworth (meaning that here we have the first variant consisting *entirely* of Soft Machine alumni) for the studio album *Abracadabra* recorded over two days live in London in June 2002 – three months before the Polysoft recording

– and a live set from a tour of Japan in August 2003 commemorated as *Abracadabra In Osaka* (2020) and two bonus tracks on a 2018 reissue of *Abracadabra*.

Here's a good place to trace Holdsworth's own meandering path since leaving Soft Machine in 1975. At first, it's not easy to see where he thought he would fit into an already oversaturated American scene where guitarists proliferated and where the standouts – everyone from John McLaughlin and Al Di Meola to Carlos Santana and Frank Zappa – had both chops and a distinctive vision. The heavy metal shred crowd had not yet emerged. Holdsworth could play, but could he be a charismatic stylist?

This may be unfair to Holdsworth, who genuinely admired Tony Williams and might have seen joining him as an artistic opportunity rather than a career move. But Holdsworth's tenure in The New Tony Williams Lifetime amounted to another apprenticeship in an entire decade of them. Holdsworth played on the excellent, solo-saturated *Believe It* (1975) and the less-inspiring *Million Dollar Legs* (1976) before – in a cruel rerun of his Soft Machine experience – the outfit ran out of money mid-tour and he was forced to scurry home. While in America, he was given the opportunity to record a solo album, but this was also a bust. He cut a bunch of demos of tricky fusion workouts, only for them to be released unpolished and seemingly without his permission as *Velvet Darkness*.

Had ambition still been the driver, rather than humiliation and lack of funds, Holdsworth would then surely *not* have bounced into another drummer's band, Gong. Daevid Allen had long gone, and even Steve Hillage had drifted away when Pierre Moerlen took Gong's reins in 1976, steering it toward wholly instrumental percussion-based fusion. Holdsworth was added on their best post-Allen album, *Gazeuse!*. It's as colourful and exuberant as its cover and as frothy as its Perrier-referencing title ('carbonated!'): cascades of marimba and vibes over which Holdsworth plays poised, careful solos, in particular the splashy note-bending of opener 'Expresso'. He toured the album with Gong, and was back for their fine second album *Expresso II* (1978) and as a guest on one track of the mediocre *Time Is The Key* (1979).

During this period, Holdsworth also dabbled in straight jazz and free improvisation, playing on drummer John Stevens's *Touching On*, with pianist Gordon Beck on *Sunbird* and their collaboration *The Things You See*, and on sets involving Softs members John Marshall and Ray Warleigh – with the latter of whom Holdsworth had played a BBC session as early as his own tenure in June 1974. He also performed with Nucleus for the BBC in 1980 (heard on the *Live At The BBC* box) and was back with Soft Machine for sessions for *Land Of Cockayne* the same year.

But next to give him a shot at the big time was fusion violinist Jean-Luc Ponty, who took Holdsworth back to the US to play guitar alongside Daryl Stuermer on Ponty's album *Enigmatic Ocean* (1977). With violin occupying a sonic space similar to the guitar – and taking the bulk of the solos – the album is dense and congested, but Holdsworth's rare spotlights glide effortlessly through the noise. Though he fled from the subsequent tour after only a handful of dates, he was back with Ponty on *Individual Choice* (1983).

Holdsworth was then drawn to yet another drummer, Bill Bruford, who invited him to play on the drummer's solo album *Feels Good To Me* (1978) and the Bruford band album *One Of A Kind* (1979). The sound of the former – pointedly, with a gong on the cover – was indeed very close to *Gazeuse!* with its layers of tuned percussion, though Bruford played in a more neurotic and spiky fashion and the jagged funk gave Holdsworth much more to work with. Too much, perhaps, since he seems overwhelmed by trying to overdub solos onto Bruford's twisted compositions, particularly when Annette Peacock is singing.

In between those two albums, Bruford formed U.K., one of the first prog rock supergroups. Originally it was intended to be a new version of King Crimson involving the Fripp/Wetton/Bruford trio that had released the highly regarded *Red* in 1974. Fripp eventually dropped the project, so Bruford replaced him with Holdsworth and added keyboardist/violinist Eddie Jobson essentially to reproduce Crimson's David Cross. The result was an eponymous album that should have set the world on fire – even Zappa expressed his admiration for Holdsworth – but in 1978, the planet wasn't ready for dinosaur superstars (unlike three years later, when John Wetton repeated the exercise with Asia). A disastrous US tour ripped U.K. to shreds and Wetton had Holdsworth fired. Various live tapes from the tour have been released, including three gigs in the massive *Ultimate Collector's Edition* box (2016).

After all this turmoil, Holdsworth finally decided to form his own band. On the eve of a 1979 tour in support of *One Of A Kind*, he walked out on Bruford exactly as he'd done with Soft Machine and Ponty. He first abortively approached Jon Hiseman and Jack Bruce, then joined a band called False Alarm (not the US punk group), and in 1982 released the solo album *I.O.U.*, which finally enabled him to crack America.

He hit his peak with the *Metal Fatigue* (1985), by which time his style was virtuoso fusion with pop vocals. Subsequently, his work was characterised by the guitar synthesizer. His last album of note before returning to the Soft Machine family was a 1996 collaboration with Gordon Beck on jazz and pop standards, *None Too Soon*.

Soft Works played a smattering of old favourites: 'Facelift', 'Kings And Queens', and 'As If' from Soft Machine, and 'Calyx' from Hatfield And The North, with Dean playing the vocal line on sax. It was an odd line-up for a band with this heritage, consisting of two lead instruments (sax and guitar), bass, and drums, but with no keyboards except when Dean doubled on Fender Rhodes. This put a great deal of the Soft Machine catalogue out of its reach, but it obviously worked since the format has endured to this day.

In effect, Soft Works's set consists mostly of standard jazz improvisation – Dean and Holdsworth taking turns emoting over smooth, unwavering backgrounds. The old pieces have a gaping sonic absence as if some inept engineer has omitted Ratledge's counterpoint, but 'As If' (retitled 'Has Riff' on *Abracadabra In Osaka*) is as heavy as an approaching thunderstorm and 'Facelift' a radical reimagining with an introduction as still as a murder scene and a noir bulk that turns hard corners in rainy black cars.

While in Japan in 2003, Dean and Hopper joined local musicians Akio 'Hoppy' Kamiyama and Yoshida Tatsuya, for a live studio session, eventually released in 2007 as *Soft Mountain*. The name alone gets it into this book. Kamiyama and Tatsuya had prior links to the Canterbury Scene. Kamiyama had played on the 1999 Gong Family 30th Anniversary tour, to which Hopper had also contributed as part of the Hopper, Daevid Allen, and Chris Cutler trio that would become Brainville 3. Prolific Ruins drummer Tatsuya played for Acid Mothers Temple, including on its shambolic 2003 collaboration with Allen as Acid Mothers Gong.

A similar experiment, Soft Bounds saw Dean and Hopper add Equipe Out pianist (and yet another Pip Pyle girlfriend) Sophia Domancich and drummer Simon Goubert for sporadic gigs in France over the next two years. They played Le Triton on 17 June 2004, releasing the results the following year as *Live At Le Triton 2004*: three lengthy new pieces of wide-ranging, mostly improvised skronk and a 16-minute rendition of 'Kings And Queens'. More from the same gig appeared on the seventh volume *Soft Boundaries* of the *Dedicated To Hugh* collection, including a sultry 24-minute 'Slightly All The Time', along with parts of a gig at Le Triton the following June. The band's final concert was a May 2006 tribute to Elton Dean, performing as a trio with a host of guests.

Jumping a little further ahead, one more offshoot is of note. Hopper guested on a short version of 'Facelift' on The Delta Saxophone Quartet's Soft Machine tribute album *Dedicated To You...But You Weren't Listening* (2007), which was enough to get his name on the front cover.

Abracadabra (2003)

Personnel:
Elton Dean: alto saxophone, saxello, electric piano
Allan Holdsworth: electric guitar, SynthAxe
Hugh Hopper: bass
John Marshall: drums
Recorded June 2002, Eastcote Studios, London, UK
Producer: Soft Works
Label: MoonJune
Release date: March 2003
Running time: 1:00:12

This is the first studio album featured in this book never to have been
released on vinyl. The covers were different in Europe and Japan. In 2018,
the album was reissued in Japan with a mini-LP sleeve (!) using the European
design and included two bonus tracks: 'Baker's Treat' and 'Alphrazallan'
recorded live on the August 2003 tour.

'Seven Formerly' (Dean, Marshall)

Holdsworth's guitar synth brings a contemporary sheen to the Dean/Hopper/
Marshall trio at its most seductive, slipping luxuriously bland down the gullet
of ten scarcely mobile minutes. Marshall's busy cascades are all a feint. Even
when Hopper plays a minimal 7/8 groove for the others to spool around,
the band seem transfixed by their own stature. The highlight is Holdsworth's
brief solo from 6:33 – gabbling plastic tones that seem to fill the room
without once announcing themselves as volume. Afterwards, Dean attempts
to emulate him, but the piece to drop away into a hazy psychedelic dub and
more of those delectable synths.

'First Trane' (Hopper)

The album's longest (at 11:35) and most immaculate piece signals its intention
right there in the title, and indeed here's an old-fashioned bop rhythm on bass
for Dean to insinuate himself around while Holdsworth plays slabs of brassy
chords. The very idea would be conceited were not Dean such a masterful
player in this lyrical style, threading effortless snippets of melody together.
The freer he gets, the more the others rally around. Even Holdsworth takes
delight in shadowing Dean's runs with chopped-up SynthAxe chords. Like a
repeat of 'Seven Formerly', Holdsworth gets the spotlight from 6:54, and this
time, the tone is pure stoner thrill. He leaps through bizarre atonal runs and
wanton guitar trickery, again lifting the piece immeasurably.

'Elsewhere' (Hopper)

It's a little disappointing to start with those same SynthAxe sweeps, but if
you're not already horizontal and mind-expanded you're missing the point.

The simple bass riff that begins 43 seconds in is as languid as the rest, and Dean slinks without much enthusiasm, but Marshall's exuberant fills increase the energy.

'K Licks' (Miller)
This is a sly tribute to Phil Miller's 'Calyx' played as a hesitant, wormy duet for Hopper's fuzz and Dean's sax, with staggers of pixie-headed accompaniment by the others. Dean finds all kinds of lysergic means to pervert the melody to the point of doing everything to his horn except jump up and down on the keys.

'Baker's Treat' (Dean)
A sultry evening where post-coital lovers lean over the balcony and drop ash in the swimming pool beneath. As you'd guess from the title, this is another Dean pastiche, and the cool-blue mood is evoked perfectly. There are a few spiky, recriminatory moments in Holdsworth's chewy-toned solo, but the sax lulls everything back to a last sleepy caress: two butts flicked like glimmering stars at the spangled L.A. night.

'Willie's Knee' (Dean)
Regal jumping jazz with plump organ chords forms the foundation for another of Holdsworth's plastic guitar runs and Dean's brightest and most swinging sax playing on the disc. It's another tribute and an even more personal one. The title refers to the saxophonist honing his craft through Willie Thomas's *Jazz Anyone.....?* books.

'Abracadabra' (Hopper, Marshall)
For the first two minutes the track stays on those familiar SynthAxe sweeps and Dean's exhausted midnight sax, but Hopper then builds another of elaborate bass riff and Dean finds sudden acreages of wall to scribble on. Marshall, too, wields his kit like an assault weapon. But the relax comes disappointingly early and there's no space for a Holdsworth solo in the entire 7:33 running time.

'Madame Vintage' (Holdsworth, Marshall)
Holdsworth's one writing credit on the album is an improvised dialogue for guitar and drums. It begins with yet more of the blurry SynthAxe swells that threaten to suck the last dregs of energy out of the album despite Marshall's manful attempt to interject percussive accents. But this is soon replaced by a roaring guitar solo set against scrabbling free runs on the drums that do actually evoke some of the old fire. The obvious corollary is the Etheridge/ Marshall duet 'The Camden Tandem' on *Softs,* but this is one errant guitarist and a whole effects rack later.

Soft Mountain (2007)

Personnel:
Elton Dean: alto saxophone
Hugh Hopper: bass
Hoppy Kamiyama: keyboards
Yoshida Tatsuya: drums
Recorded 10 August 2003, Gok Sound, Tokyo, Japan
Producer: Soft Mountain
Label: Hux
Released date: UK: January 2007
Running time: 58:38

The CD has been issued only once, and there was no vinyl version.

'Soft Mountain Suite Pt. 1' (Dean, Hopper, Kamiyama, Tatsuya)
'Soft Mountain Suite Pt. 2' (Dean, Hopper, Kamiyama, Tatsuya)
If Hopper's liner notes are correct, and the band simply arrived at the studio
with no material and went at it with no discussion, 'head down and wailing
completely improvised for 45 minutes' for the first piece, then 'had a short
drinks break and then did another 45' for the second, what we have are
excerpts: 30:44 of the first and 27:54 of the second. I doubt there was much
in the way of editing within the body of the pieces, if editing squally-free jazz
is even possible. There are fades on three of the four endings.
    The point of the session was for Hopper and Dean to shake loose creatively
in the middle of a tour hidebound by its setlist. This is basically all you need
to know. The mix isn't good. It has a boxy ambience that distances the grand
piano, turns the drums to a sludgy mess of clumps and clangs, and makes
caverns out of Hopper's bass. But Dean's sax cuts through all the deficiencies,
and there's a lot of energy in that space.
    Tatsuya is firmly of the Phil Howard mould. Hopper has apparently
mellowed into acceptance of the chaos, and putters along with crazed runs
and long stretches of throbbing fuzz monotones and Can-style grooves. The
disappointment is Kamiyama, who is no Ratledge even when he switches to
an amplified instrument. He seems lost during his features. He can certainly
play – in an unaccompanied solo near the album's end, he adeptly strings
together cascades of quasi-classical runs – but he doesn't gel with the others.
The lengthy, plain noise sections at least give him the excuse to pound
mallet-like at the keys.
    Kamiyama does interject some yelping vocals, electronic frippery, and Holger
Czukay-style found sounds here and there, but I wish I could hear a mix of
the other three players without him. All the best stretches are when Kamiyama
shuts up or disappears into the background. The most effective parts are when
Hopper and Tatsuya hammer at each other in long, frenetic duets, a format in
which Tatsuya, of course, is right at home since it's the format of Ruins.

The album's major problem is that both parts are the same. It would have been far better to smash about like teenagers in one part and try circling each other softly like adults in the other – the format of an early Ash Ra Tempel album, say. Still, Ruins fans will adore the pummelling, and a few of the more manic excerpts would definitely have benefited some of the later Soft Machine albums. Get in the right mood and play the disc loud enough and it sure does make your room hop, and at its not insubstantial heights – about halfway through the second part, say, when Hopper and Tatsuya lock into a mutated caveman funk – it could easily lift your whole building off its feet.

Soft Machine Legacy And The Return of the Name

Those who tally the dead already know where this is headed because the shadows have long since settled over these pages. As I write this in 2023, Ratledge and Wyatt are the only original members of Soft Machine still with us. The Canterbury dynasty has depleted, as all dynasties do. We lost Alan Gowen and Gary Windo long ago. Elton Dean and Pip Pyle died in 2006, Hugh Hopper in 2009, Lol Coxhill in 2012, Kevin Ayers and Richard Coughlan in 2013, Daevid Allen and Ray Warleigh (leaving separately but together, just as they joined us) in 2015, Allan Holdsworth and Phil Miller in 2017, and Keith Tippett in 2020.

Their music survives only if it's played, and the best way to ensure that is through live performers bringing the sounds to new ears. Daevid Allen understood this when he organised Gong not as one man's fossil but as an ever-changing continuity of players in the here and now. The rolling boil of Soft Machine's personnel is much the same. The band passed from Allen's hands the moment he left in September 1967, and has moved through a succession of other hands since. Those who continue the Soft Machine name do not do so to revere a single person or uphold a single sound. They bring a floating flux of inspiration and feeling that carries all the earlier work with them into the future.

With all that in mind, the most important change in the band's history occurred in 2004. Soft Works had continued to play occasional gigs that year, but any momentum ceased when Holdsworth quit. The others replaced him, just as before, with John Etheridge. In contrast to that huge Holdsworth resume that I listed earlier, Etheridge had had a reasonably quiet two decades after the run of final Softs shows at Ronnie Scott's in 1984. He continued to work with Stéphane Grappelli and played in the shadow of a number of many better-known musicians, including John Williams, Danny Thompson, Nigel Kennedy, and Andy Summers. You could have wiped Etheridge's name from much of this work and the world wouldn't have cared. Elton Dean had recorded with Etheridge in 1995, so he was a logical choice and effectively the *only* choice for a guitarist with direct Soft Machine pedigree, though it's a curious fact that Hopper and Etheridge had never performed together before 2004 despite having been in the same band.

For the next iteration of the name, the quartet cut straight to the quick with 'The Soft Machine Legacy' (divested – like the parent – of its definite article after the first couple of releases). Whether or not it infringed a trademark, the identifier could be used with creative typesetting to suggest live shows were closer-related to the old band than they actually were, and to avoid any hint that this was a tribute act. The same sleight-of-hand was employed on the cover of all but one of the band's releases: placing 'Soft Machine' on one line and 'Legacy' on the next so it looked like an album called *Legacy* by Soft Machine (the untitled first studio album and *Live In Zaandam*), writing 'Soft Machine' in large white letters and 'Legacy' in smaller, less visible letters (*Live*

At The New Morning and *Live Adventures*), and setting 'Legacy' in a different colour so it faded into the design (*Steam*).

The Dean/Etheridge/Hopper/Marshall quartet released two official live recordings, *Live In Zaandam* (2005) from De Kade, Zaandam, Holland on 10 May 2005, and *Live At The New Morning* (2006) from New Morning, Paris, on 12 December 2005. They also recorded a studio album over two days that September. As with Soft Works, the bulk of the live set was new material, but there was space for a few Soft Machine pieces in their now-familiar new formats: 'Kings And Queens', 'As If', and 'Facelift'.

Live In Zaandam – a document of the band's first gig together – sets out as relaxed a stall as *Softs* from Etheridge's gliding opener 'Ash' (originally on his 1994 album of that title) through the Sunday morning chill-out of 'Baker's Treat' to a 'Kings And Queens' so comfy the band seems to be playing it face-down on massage benches. '1212' is the only track destined for the studio. (It's pronounced 'one two one two' but given on different releases of the studio album as 'Twelve Twelve' or '12/12'.) The piece fixates on a slinky unison line by Dean and Etheridge before spitting out fur balls of competing solos. But the players rouse themselves for a brief guitar/drums workout 'Two Down' (the son of the son of 'The Camden Tandem') and the funky Etheridge piece 'Big Creese'.

Live At The New Morning bookends the quartet at the end of its run. Everything is longer, chunkier, and more confident, including a soaring phase effect on a monumental 'Ash' that is largely a showcase for Etheridge's and Hopper's effect racks, a diversion into gloopy psychedelic guitar on a new version of Dean's 'Seven For Lee', and Etheridge playing to his effects in an 'As if' (again here as 'Has Riff') that slowly climbs to demonic peaks. Dean's entry startles the whole room. Marshall's drum feature 'Sideburn' (it's less than five minutes long) moves straight into 'Two Down', his duet with Etheridge's strings abuse, and then into the studio disc's 'Kite Runner', the most disjointed James Brown impersonation since Led Zeppelin's 'The Crunge'.

But the real surprise of the set is that both Hopper and Etheridge chat to the audience between numbers, something we've never heard on an official live outing before. It's just not cricket to have to deal with a Soft Machine that seem so happy with themselves and each other to the point of Hopper giving an affectionate shout-out to his partner Christine.

The performance was filmed for the DVD *New Morning: The Paris Concert* (2006). The greatest joy here is seeing Dean and Hopper at the last peak of their prime, as gnarly and crumpled as their clothes, but the camera also gives us a masterclass in Etheridge's playing. Watch for the way he defies his strings to ring out in 'Kite Runner'.

A change in personnel was now imposed on the band by more than mere internal animosity. When Dean's health failed in 2006, his slot was much harder to fill. The others turned to ex-Gong woodwind player Theo Travis, a man 20 years younger than the others. Of the huge number of collaborations and projects he'd worked on – including playing with John Marshall, David Sinclair, Robert Fripp, Dick Heckstall-Smith, Steven Wilson, and many others – perhaps the most inviting to readers is Jade Warrior's *Distant Echoes* (1993) on which he joined flautist Jon Field and guests including King Crimson violinist David Cross. Though Jade Warrior were a shadow of the band they used to be, *Distant Echoes* is still a wondrous mix of shimmering fusion and world music. It's an entry into a catalogue well worth exploring.

The new Soft Machine quartet was immortalised on a studio album *Steam* (2007), recorded over three days at Jon Hiseman's studio in December 2006.

Hugh Hopper's own health issues – he, like Gowen, was to succumb to leukaemia – caused the band to turn to his In Cahoots colleague Fred Thelonious Baker to deputise, and then to old friend Roy Babbington for a permanent replacement. Babbington's activity since we last heard from him in 1976 is of less relevance to readers – mostly straight jazz but also recording stints with City Boy, Elvis Costello, and Madeline Bell, among others. After what was essentially a try-out as Soft Trio with Etheridge and Marshall, Babbington joined the band for real in October 2008. The result was a Soft Machine reunion that contained three of the five players that had made *Softs* in 1976.

This line-up documented their live work on *Live Adventures* (2010), recorded over two nights in October 2009 in Linz, Austria and Habach, Germany. Though the electronic effects rob the music of its intimacy in pursuit of the gloss of Gong's latter-day reinvention as new-age trance spiritualists, if you peer through them, you'll find a band leaning on the delicate expressivity of flute for the first time since 1970. Travis uses it brilliantly as foil and counterpoint to Etheridge's spikier tone. The sax – which takes over for all but two numbers – is best used in unison lines with the guitar as on 'Grape Hound' and 'The Nodder', leaving Etheridge to provide the solo fire that lifts every track he's let loose on, in particular, his one-man exuberance on 'Gesolreut'.

In August 2012, the band recorded the studio album *Burden Of Proof* (2013). Seventeen minutes of a performance the following September at the Rock In Opposition Festival in Carmaux, France (with occasional sub Mark Fletcher on drums) were used in the *Romantic Warriors III* companion DVD *Got Canterbury?* (2016). A brief but lovely 'Chloe And The Pirates' is the highlight.

In 2015, the band succumbed to the inevitable and dropped the 'Legacy' from their name, meaning that promoters no longer had to feign their way around it even if they'd bothered in the first place.

Over three days in December 2017, Soft Machine returned to Jon Hiseman's studio to record *Hidden Details* (2018) and, as if to underscore the defiance of that release, used the *Third* font (Epic Shaded) for the cover of *Live At The Baked Potato* (2020) recorded on 1 February 2019 at the famous L.A. jazz venue. (Epic Shaded also graces 2023's *Other Doors*, so I guess it's now considered as Soft Machine branding.) *Live At The Baked Potato* adroitly balances old and new, but notably, there are no longueurs at all. The longest track is barely over seven minutes. Even the old material is played without fuss or showboating, which may disappoint you if you yearn for the unpredictability of a 'Facelift' organ introduction or even some free-jazz whiplash. Most of all, the set is arranged and played like a rock show, with what is effectively walk-on music in the Proms-evoking 'Out-Bloody-Rageous' keyboard patterns, a sound effects tape to herald 'Hazard Profile', and properly mapped-out arrangements that are followed diligently. Even Etheridge's guitar outbursts on 'The Tale Of Taliesin' seem scripted – the very thing Soft Mountain had rebelled against.

Babbington retired in 2021 and was replaced full-time by Fred Thelonious Baker, another sprightly young wisp of a man at just 61 years of age when he joined. Baker's pedigree included a long stint in Phil Miller's band In Cahoots (as Hugh Hopper's replacement), playing alongside Elon Dean and Pip Pyle. As well as Baker's recorded work with Miller, there were a brace of solo albums and the intriguing project *One Take* (2010) on which he performed with John Marshall.

After recording *Other Doors* – their second studio album as Soft Machine – Marshall also embarked on a well-earned retirement. He is the longest-serving and dare I say, best of all the band's drummers. The stool is now home to the positively baby-faced Asaf Sirkis, who may well prove himself better still. With an average age of just 63, we can hopefully expect a more adventurous repertoire drawn from the entire history of the band for years to come. Pick a page at random from this book, guys, and stab your finger at a title. Soft Machine, as a living heritage to be reinvented, certainly has gems in plenty still to mine.

(The) Soft Machine Legacy (2006)

Personnel:
Elton Dean: alto saxophone, saxello, keyboards, percussion
John Etheridge: electric guitar
Hugh Hopper: bass
John Marshall: drums
Recorded September 2005, Eastcote Studios, London, UK
Producer: Soft Machine Legacy
Label: MoonJune
Release date: March 2006
Running time: 57:26

Like *Abracadabra*, this album has never been released on vinyl and has had
only one reissue: in Japan in 2014, in a mini-LP sleeve. There were no bonus
tracks. Also, like *Abracadabra*, a different cover design was used in the
original 2005 Japan issue. The Europe and US versions both have a cartoon
of a clockwork car with the lettering 'Soft Machine Legacy' in yellow. The
Japan version has a far superior collage of machine parts, breast-like oranges
and bare buttocks, and is labelled 'The Soft Machine Legacy' throughout. It
also contains an insert sheet in which all four members provide handwritten
greetings to their Japanese fans. Disappointingly, the 2014 issue uses the
clockwork car design but with the lettering in red.

'Kite Runner' (Etheridge)
Swooping out of silence like a heavy metal anthem, it's not until Dean's
saxes come in that you realise 'Kite Runner' is actually a species of amped-
up jazz rock. Soft Machine had certainly never been so forceful before nor
so commercially aware. Etheridge's solo is a long, masterful concatenation
of rock star tropes and poses, Dean's a swaggering walk through 20 years
of funk chops. The whole seven-minute track feels fresh and invigorating,
making the decision to fade it out a real shame.

'Ratlift' (Ratledge, Dean, Etheridge, Hopper, Marshall)
Marshall spends the first minute introducing us to every hittable surface
of his kit, and doesn't stop thrashing even when the others insinuate
themselves into the piece with Hopper's mesmerising riff, Dean's soft
Rhodes chords, and Etheridge's angle-grinding guitar hero theatrics. At
5:54, all that improvised slinking around converges into a rendition of the
'Facelift' theme played in outrageous unison. So that's the 'lift' part of the
title. Where 'Facelift' usually ends – or inverts itself on *Third* – here it slops
onward (at 6:32) into Ratledge's 'Slightly All The Time' riff played as a
vehicle for gleaming guitar harmonics and fleecy electric piano. This is so
good the fade that follows is another disappointment. It's all gone within
eight remarkable minutes.

'Twelve Twelve' (Hopper)
Hopper's back. This late-career masterpiece is a ten-minute peak. The brooding opening, like the theme to a science fiction thriller movie, zaps starry glimmers across a velvet backdrop of backwards tapes. Etheridge's guitar is bright and lonely as a falling star. The piece that develops casts Dean at his most hesitant, adrift against clusters of riffs and a remarkably restrained Marshall. There's the finest meandering theme I've heard since the heights of the old days. And best of all: the track *wants* to wrongfoot you, shifting gears as if at random so that you spend the bulk of the piece spooked in by the most otherworldly of sonic shadows. Even an inversion into sunshine is deceptive, for Etheridge's solo feature is a drool-jawed killer.

'F & I' (Dean, Etheridge)
This short, extraordinary quarrel between Etheridge's fiery guitar and Dean's icy electric piano is all jump and recoil, flinging in jazz and funk motifs and then dancing away before they can land.

'Fresh Brew' (Dean, Etheridge, Hopper, Marshall)
A back-porch creeper bass sets the mood for the improvisation, prompting wide-eyed cat stares from Dean's sax and rainy-night window taps from Marshall's kit. Etheridge bellows and squeals like passing trucks. As the atmosphere intensifies, it's as if we're witness to an escalating psychosis played out as an inner struggle to retain control. I reckon two of these players are saying, 'look what *we* could have done with the Soft Mountain tape'. There's certainly a lot more agility here, the sense that the piece could – and does – go anywhere it likes, from comic swagger to knife-attack brutality. The four men listen, react, control and release, again and again. There's even something new in the breakdown.

'New Day' (Dean)
In contrast, *this* squall is Dean having almost four minutes of fun directing the others in obscene nightclub jazz. In passing, Etheridge channels a host of fusion shredders and then lays them all flat.

'Fur Edge' (Dean, Marshall)
This is the only suite on the disc. After 3:48 of 'New Day' we subside into this scurrying hedgerow collision of drums and sax, like a mole's monumental life-or-death struggle with a worm.

'Theta Meter' (Dean, Hopper)
At 6:36, the suite's final part announces itself in a Neanderthal drum rhythm to mushroom-headed whorls of electronics and layered, disconnected bass lines. Here it remains until at 10:18, it hisses off into the annihilating gape of the cosmos.

'Grape Hound' (Etheridge)

Etheridge gets to drive the music again at the end of the album, just as he did at the opening. Once more, his conception of the Legacy is heavy rock, sounding a lot like the last firing neurones of a massively chemicalised Cream during the 20th minute of a particularly brutal live 'Born Under A Bad Sign' in 1968. Hopper handles the knots of the riff with aplomb. From 2:50, the piece begins to collapse, but roadies rush in to prop up the players and they manhandle themselves back to a superbly jamming second half.

'Strange Comforts' (Etheridge)

This extraordinary album, a most welcome return to form, concludes with a change of pace. For 1:19, there's just Etheridge's electric guitar at its gentlest and most lyrical, and it would have been enough had it ended there. Instead, we get a reedy saxello theme and a further five minutes of settle-down jazz rhythms from Hopper and Marshall over which the guitarist unwinds the most elegant of improvisations.

Steam (2007)

Personnel:
John Etheridge: electric guitar
Hugh Hopper: bass
John Marshall: drums
Theo Travis: saxophones, flute
Recorded December 2006, Temple Music Studio, Sutton, UK
Producer: Soft Machine Legacy
Label: MoonJune
Release date: 2007
Running time: 1:05:34

Steam was another album never released on vinyl. It came with a cover sticker that titled the band 'Soft Machine (Legacy)'. There was one reissue in 2014, the now-expected Japan mini-LP sleeve.

'Footloose' (Hopper)
Despite the goodtime vibe of the track's title, *Steam* opens in a haunted place, channelling unpleasant memories. Hopper's angular bass theme feels like something hemmed in by enemies, in particular Marshall's threatening drum clatter, and Etheridge doesn't know what to do with his solo so leans on dissonant up and down runs and pedal gloop. At 8:44, 'Footloose' is the longest track of an album that carefully delineates Soft Machine into its various compartments, old and new – there are no suites – but seems to have forgotten how these parts once slotted together into the momentum it advertises.

'The Steamer' (Travis)
In this jumpy, energetic workout, Travis throws in cascades of awkward jazzy rhythms for the others to negotiate. Etheridge is again burdened by effects, but occasionally comes up with suitable twitchy phrases. Hopper and Marshall count dutifully through the piece but neither seems engaged by it.

'The Big Man' (Etheridge, Hopper, Marshall, Travis)
A monstrous grunge drone forms an incongruous backing for Travis's frantic sax runs. Marshall pounds, stumbles, pounds, stumbles. Etheridge delights in his broken-backed death-metal grunting and lightning arpeggios that are so buried in the squall it's like you're hearing them through a bedroom wall with a head full of flu. But there's something unfinished about all this nastiness, something not quite said.

'Chloe And The Pirates' (Ratledge)
The vibe fares much better on this sumptuous reworking of an old delight, which even comes with slurps of backwards guitar throughout. Travis

141

enunciates the theme clearly on the silkiest of sax tones, and neither soloist tries to dominate in lilting, sensitive features.

'In The Back Room' (Etheridge)

Etheridge's spot is the kind of creepy-crawly jazz that a spider combo might play under the stairs for a dance floor of obliviously goggle-eyed flies. There are humorous slides up to an innocuous swing and the makings of a shuffle drum solo before the guitarist's penetrating solo reels those suckers home. Travis's gleeful response sounds like a fat, mocking, wriggle-legged coda.

'The Last Day' (Travis)

An apocalypse of crashed teapots with ashy fuzz and burrs of flute, 'The Last Day' spends its first three minutes trying to sound like a horror-loop collage in Hopper's *1984* style. But Marshall does eventually impose structure on the chaos, after which it's largely Etheridge's show, both in his nastiest squalls and in dominating Travis's theme. The piece then expends itself on a very long decay that ought to have been the prelude to something bigger and far more significant – a noise epic the band seem perplexingly unqualified to deliver.

'Firefly' (Hopper, Marshall)

Travis's opportunity to show what his flute-playing brings to the band jousts with one of Hopper's patent avant-garde loop structures but is dispensed far too quickly in favour of a Marshall solo punctuated by ensemble fanfares and the all-too-familiar straight-jazz vehicle for Etheridge's guitar. Travis returns in the tail of the piece, as well as those loops, but it all feels unconvincing and the ending is a mess.

'So English' (Etheridge, Hopper, Marshall, Travis)

This second layered band improvisation comes across like an eight-minute repeat of 'The Big Man', right down to the fuzzy grumbles and head congestion, except we're now *two* rooms away and someone in here is trying to rip up our floorboards with a petrol-driven cultivator.

'Dave Acto' (Etheridge, Hopper, Marshall, Travis)

And then they do it again, only this time it's up close and threatening – a nightmare of dentist-drill guitar and shrill saxophone. At 2:18, Etheridge coaxes the others into a blustering blues, but this, in turn, grows ever more discordant and macabre.

'Anything To Anywhere' (Travis)

As if to calm your fractured nerves after all that torment, the album ends with a bright jumping bop over which Travis layers soft, dreamy sax lines and Etheridge plays a restrained solo.

Burden Of Proof (2013)

Personnel:
Roy Babbington: bass
John Etheridge: electric guitar
John Marshall: drums
Theo Travis: tenor saxophone, flute, keyboards
Recorded August 2012, Electromantic Studio, San Sebastiano Da Pó, Italy
Producer: Soft Machine Legacy
Label: MoonJune
Release date: 2013
Running time: 55:07

Released on CD only and not reissued so far.

'Burden Of Proof' (Etheridge)
As if to demonstrate the legitimacy in the title, there's an introductory minute of softly cascading electric piano patterns in the gentlest washes of delay. The piece proper is a humorously confident strut to which Etheridge and Travis play an archetypal Soft Machine theme in tight unison. Each takes a solo to Babbington's dancing bass and Marshall's restless snare.

'Voyage Beyond Seven' (Travis)
In this complex Softs-meet-Gong psychedelic excursion, fidgety motifs lead into a loose duet for sax and guitar, a long Etheridge loop improvisation with shadowy flute and snowy spatters of rhythm, a full-on band apocalypse, and a bolted-on fanfare ending.

'Kitto' (Etheridge)
This is slightly under two minutes of moody solo guitar, again with loop effects. Assuming that's a Japanese title, it merely means 'certainly' and therefore fits with a band that gave us 'Virtually' and 'Slightly All The Time'.

'Pie Chart' (Etherbidge)
Against a slow pedestrian blues, Travis tackles that dead-end sax that Dean used to do so well, but with mixed results. He has the right tone, but he injects some inappropriate moments of raunch that you'd never associate with Dean's tighter, more wiry sound world. Etheridge's solo is exactly what you'd expect, merging wild runs and anthemic highs. The piece fades while the pair are carving up sections of dialogue like the slices of the title.

'JSP' (Marshall)
A restrained one-minute kit and gong solo from the man who also brought us 'L B O' and 'D.I.S.'

143

'Kings And Queens' (Hopper)
Like the two Legacy albums that precede it, *Burden Of Proof* finds space for a solitary rework of an old theme, in this case, the delectable moment of drift in the middle of side one of *Fourth*.

This rendition may be intended as a tribute to their latest lost colleague, but the band find ways to update and deepen the sound, with pillows of electronic shimmer, a yearning and deeply heartfelt solo by Etheridge, and lovely echo flute by Travis.

'Fallout' (Travis)
The album's longest singleton is something of a shambles. It's lumbered both with a Gong-style title and a Gong-style meandering sax riff, and consists mostly of a Gong-style sonic meltdown and trip sequence to which you can well imagine Daevid Allen swaying around the stage. The band make all the required noises, but it's not in the least bit mind-expanding and I don't think Babbington enjoys it one jot.

'Going Somewhere Canorous?' (Babbington, Marshall)
Another minute-long feature, this effect-laden bass improvisation set to disconnected cymbals, isn't quite as melodic as the title suggests but does evoke a fistful of fragments of Jade Warrior.

'Black And Crimson' (Travis)
There's a touch of Karl Jenkins at his most formal in this puffy electric piano riff and simple guitar theme, and neither soloist put much heart in it, but the rhythm is tricky enough to hold the attention for the five minutes it rolls along.

'The Brief' (Marshall, Travis)
The album's only suite begins with two and a half minutes of Marshall bluster and Didier Malherbe-like sax skronk.

'Pump Room' (Etheridge)
The concluding section is one of those metal rock workouts that were such an arresting feature of *Soft Machine Legacy*, but it's played too muted and clean to be as convincing. The highlight is a grinding guitar solo to Babbington's hardest poses, but even here Etheridge's effects rob the tone of its power.

'Green Cubes' (Babbington, Etheridge, Marshall, Travis)
Five more minutes of loop exposition that again sounds like a Gong improvisation. At 3:42, a jaunty funk rhythm feels for all the world like we're about to cascade into that band's 'Flying Teapot'. Instead, Etheridge solos into the cop-out of a fade.

'They Landed On A Hill' (Etheridge, Travis)
The album ends back in the rippling electric piano space of the opener,
accompanied by Etheridge's tranquil lines.

Hidden Details (2018)

Personnel:
Roy Babbington: bass
John Etheridge: electric and acoustic guitar
John Marshall: drums
Theo Travis: saxophones, flute, keyboards
Nick Utteridge: wind chimes
Recorded December 2017, Temple Music Studio, Sutton, UK
Producers: Theo Travis, John Etheridge
Label: MoonJune
Release date: September 2018
Running time: 59:55

It appears that the return of the Soft Machine name warranted an extensive release program for this album, always with the same front cover. The original album was issued in the same month on a MoonJune CD and a 'deluxe' double non-gatefold LP on Tonefloat Records. The LPs came on a choice of black, orange, blue, or marbled vinyl, the colours all in very limited quantities. The result was the expected media attention by reviewers that had ignored the Legacy band for years, and an uptick in sales. There have been no reissues since.

The track lengths and running order of the LP are identical to the CD: tracks 1–3 (total time 17:57) on side one, tracks 4–9 on side two (20:36), and tracks 10–13 on side three (21:19). However, the LP also includes an additional track 'Night Sky' at the end of side one, taking its running time up to 21:12. On the Japanese CD alone, 'Night Sky' was added to the end of the disc as a 'bonus track' after 30 seconds of silence. The distinction is therefore important, since the CDs in all territories had space to include the track – and of course, they all could have sequenced it after 'Ground Lift'. Additionally, they could have included much of the further 19:40 of lesser material that filled the fourth side of the vinyl (omitting, let's say, an alternative take of 'Ground Lift').

'Hidden Details' (Travis)
Etheridge's guitar grounds the title track in a rough-hewn King Crimson style of math rock. Babbington adds a dependably brutal counterpoint, but the others distance the piece from accusations of metal pandering. Marshall plays a skittery jazz rhythm, and Travis's sax is slinky, elegant, and utterly inappropriate. It's likely that the dichotomy was the point – to show that this band, like the one whose name they took, had agile chops but were as hard as a kick in the teeth.

'The Man Who Waved At Trains' (Ratledge)
The first of the album's two backward nods is as glowingly pleasurable as the *Bundles* original. This time, the duet is Travis's smiling flute and Etheridge's

slightly sour guitar tone. Speckles of the now-familiar echo on electric piano and the flute add subtle lysergic touches, sonic receptivity among modern listeners for what is at heart a thoroughly old-fashioned jazz vamp.

'Ground Lift' (Travis, Babbington)
Against a springy industrial ambience, the band plays a leisurely improvisation of guitar spirals and ethnic sax that takes more than half the five-minute running time to coalesce. Even then, it refuses to do more than sidestep dramatically on lumbering chords and Travis's spikiest blasts.

'Heart Off Guard' (Etheridge)
For a full minute at the start of this suite opener, Etheridge plays the first acoustic guitar we've heard in the Legacy years. His picking is bright and warm, but there are none of the virtuoso flights of 'Etika' on *Softs* – it merely marks time. For the rest, Travis plays smoky sax over the top, which the title presumably wants you to associate with lost love and solitary evenings in the bedsit of the soul.

'Broken Hill' (Etheridge)
The final suspended note of 'Heart Off Guard' decays at 2:30 into this teary electric guitar ballad featuring four full minutes of Etheridge at his most sumptuous. His blues playing is poised and fully in control of its emotional impact.

'Flight Of The Jett' (Marshall, Travis, Etheridge, Babbington)
This two-minute improvisation is heavy on Marshall's kit excursions to which Travis and Etheridge provide only glowers of electric piano and disconnected guitar. I don't hear anything from Babbington, regardless of his credit. The 'hidden detail' of the album title might be the way the CD and LP list the composition credits differently. I've chosen the LP version as feeling more correct. It's Etheridge, Travis, Marshall, Babbington on the CD, which is surely wrong.

'One Glove' (Etheridge)
A pleasingly disjointed funk rhythm drives this fine ensemble workout in which Etheridge dons his figurative leather jacket one more time. During the times when Travis stops playing his jazzy sax, the track is the album's most interesting sound sculpture: a tangled rock trio butting just enough machismo against each other to thicken your space with manly swagger.

'Out Bloody Intro' (Travis, Ratledge)
The second Soft Machine cover starts with almost three minutes of softly pealing electric piano played largely as layered real-time lines rather than the loops of the original. They're all variations on Ratledge's original (or Hopper's

original, if you want to be pedantic), meaning this could easily have been merged into 'Out-Bloody-Rageous' proper without requiring Travis's nod.

'Out-Bloody-Rageous (Part 1)' (Ratledge)
All is fully in place in this faithful five-minute rendition of the main theme, though it's a little disconcerting to hear Etheridge's guitar in this context. The bulk of the piece is taken up with a Travis sax solo in place of Ratledge's original organ run. The 'Part 1' designation makes no sense whatsoever. This section was what was generally meant by 'Out-Bloody-Rageous' when played live, and if you want to carve up the original studio construct, then surely it ought to be 'Part 2'.

'Drifting White' (Etheridge)
Consisting of shimmering solo electric guitar for slightly less than two minutes, this piece functions as the introduction to a suite since 'Life On Bridges' begins while its reverb is still fading away.

'Life On Bridges' (Travis)
The album's longest single track (8:05) begins with a sultry unison line for guitar and sax as convoluted as a Hopper theme before Babbington's fuzz follows along and Marshall skids all over the mood like he's Robert Wyatt in a strop. A muscular improvisation then stretches the piece to sinewy scar lines in which Travis's looped flutes do their best to temper the rage in Etheridge's bull-run guitar and Marshall's blind-boxer fills. It escalates into nuclear meltdown and rampaging monsters from the cracks of doom before the return of the theme brings things to a hilarious cinematic pomp of a close.

'Fourteen Hour Dream' (Travis)
The hippie signalling of the title – for sure, The Soft Machine *did* play the 14 Hour Technicolor Dream at London's Alexandra Palace in April 1967, though I doubt a two-year-old Theo Travis attended – is appropriate as the music is a fun summer-of-love pastiche complete with a descending bass line just a whisker away from Pink Floyd's *Steptoe And Son* riff on 'Interstellar Overdrive'. All the shifts are here, cunningly organised: little strident military motifs, blurry head-swaying stretches, even that *de rigueur* slow down just before the theme kicks in again.

'Breathe' (Travis, Marshall)
Nick Utteridge's capiz-shell clatter forms the background wash for more than five minutes of flute drones and paddling runs set to Marshall's swishes, gong rolls, cymbal strokes, and burbles of tympani.

'Night Sky' (Etheridge, Travis, Babbington)
The bonus track wafts Travis's flute playing over a melange of slinky guitar, bass, and flute loops accented by Etheridge's subtle phrases.

Other Doors (2023)

Personnel:
Roy Babbington, Fred Thelonious Baker: bass
John Etheridge: electric and acoustic guitar
John Marshall: drums
Theo Travis: saxophones, flute, keyboards
Recorded July–August 2022, Temple Music Studio, Sutton, UK
Producers: Theo Travis, John Etheridge
Label: MoonJune
Release date: June 2023
Running time: 56:26

John Marshall's final release with the band was also a fond farewell to
Roy Babbington, who guests on two tracks. Like *Hidden Details*, the CD
documented here appears to be the standard version, but limited-edition
'deluxe' double LPs on Tonefloat Records (on turquoise, green, and marbled
vinyl) again added one extra track and a fourth side of other material,
including an alternative take of 'Fell To Earth'. The extra track is a rendition
of 'Backwards'/'Noisette' that on vinyl precedes 'The Visitor At The Window'
as the first track on side three. Again, there was room for it to have been on
the standard CD had the band wanted.

'Careless Eyes' (Travis, Etheridge)
The most sumptuous world-music introduction pulls back cinematically on
thick air drones and quiet cascades of electric piano to which Travis and
Etheridge trade lilting passages on bamboo flute and electric guitar. There's
enough of the 'Shine On You Crazy Diamond' vibe for the homage to have
been purposeful. At the very least, the point is to signal the same thing
as Pink Floyd's opener: settle down, 'Careless Eyes' tells us, relax, and be
receptive, for this album is going to take you to extraordinary places.

'Penny Hitch' (Jenkins)
In the album's only segue, 'Careless Eyes' has almost faded away at 2:28
when it veers into the set's greatest surprise. From their earliest Legacy days,
the Soft Machine revival had always featured Jenkins compositions live, but
this was the first time one had appeared on a Softs studio release since 1981,
and the nod was long overdue. Jenkins wasn't just integral to the band for
many years: he left behind a host of excellent compositions that it would be
a crime to pass over forever – and besides, whatever rancour existed 50 years
ago is now long obsolete.

From Marshall's stately, dramatic fills to Babbington's plunging bass line,
the direct link to *Seven* provides a satisfying continuity right here at the
end of both men's tenure, but this is far from a carbon copy. It's Baker who
introduces the melody on swoops of fretless bass, blending with Travis's

149

elegantly restrained sax, and Etheridge who provides the climactic solo over billows of bass fuzz. But yes, the original's pause is present, and that stoned grin I mentioned way back when is slapped back on your face for good.

'Other Doors' (Etheridge)

The guitarist strikes a series of math rock angles to which Travis adds a humanising sax tone, signalling both sophistication and connection – this contemporary incarnation's trademark device. Etheridge's lengthy first-half solo is again the feature, but there's also room for Travis's sax to accumulate excitement in the second.

'Crooked Usage' (Travis)

The album's most substantial singleton (8:26) plays head games of the highest order without once coalescing into a groove. Along the way, it passes through languid but tight-plotted ensemble phrases against Marshall's cymbal washes, brooding end-of-evening pixie swagger over which Etheridge hangs spectral guitar lines, close-packed whirls of flute, tightly corralled guitar meltdown, and long hovering stretches of freeform improvisation like the pillow-thumping of a hyperactive insomniac straining for sleep. When the ensemble phrases return, they're transformed into macabre sideways lurches rife with passing danger, a drunk's dancing in the central reservation of the mind.

'Joy Of A Toy' (Ayers, Ratledge)

How do you update something this venerable and beloved? The 2022 Soft Machine manage it by slyly locating the piece *just this side* of Henri Mancini's Pink Panther theme. Etheridge stomps on the wah-wah and Baker has immense fun with the melody before the quartet pound together on the climactic chords. At last, then, we have the childlike release signalled by the title, and I bet this arrangement is going to fly on stage.

'A Flock Of Holes' (Travis, Marshall)

Over Marshall's free playing, the track hovers more of the sultry bamboo flute of the opener, this time set in braids of loop. The title is likely a reference to a flute's tone holes, though there's also an appropriate link back to Gong's 'A Sprinkling Of Clouds' on *You*, which has a similar sound toward the end.

'Whisper Back' (Etheridge)

Etheridge's solo feature interweaves clean jazz clusters with a subtle bottom-string counterpoint.

'The Stars Apart' (Etheridge)

This is sensuous jazz rock to a swaying 6/8 rhythm against which Baker and Etheridge take finely crafted solos. Travis seems content merely to play the changes on electric piano.

'Now! Is The Time' (Babbington, Baker)

It's what you expect, only a great deal better than you might fear, and a true highlight of the disc. There's a jumping enjoyment between the two bass players as they goad each other in unison and contrasting lines that makes me wish they'd teamed up for far more than just this two-minute feature.

'Fell To Earth' (Travis)

On CD, the last 20 minutes of the album are Travis compositions, forming a summary of all he brought to the band since 2006. If Etheridge is the last continuity link to the 1970s peak, Travis is surely Soft Machine's guarantee of peaks to come, ideally as part of the teamwork displayed here between a guitarist still at the height of his power and a woodwind player just coming into his. But it's the ensemble that matters, just as it always has been, even in the days when Jenkins dominated. The players lock in place as parts of what the band's name signifies, listening, reacting, encouraging, and growing together.

This brooding nose-following noir condenses everything remarkable about the current Soft Machine into slightly under six close-packed minutes – as ferocious in its compression as a Ratledge piece such as 'Teeth' but played with such swagger you never feel it exhausts its creators.

The head/variations/improv/head structure was standard by this point, but it's the invention each player brings to every part of the journey that makes it unique. The piece propels Travis's sinew-pulling sax part along a disconcerting urban groove before erupting outwards into a fabulous psychedelic monstrosity of bat-winged flutes, cruel chiming guitar, and a fuzz bass barrage so smothering you can sense Baker's delight as he plucks fragments of comedy out of the horror. Survive this, and from four minutes in you're rewarded with some of the loveliest playing the band have ever performed.

And the title? Surely there's a little humour there, too, Travis referencing his near-namesake Walter Tevis (writer of *The Man Who Fell to Earth*) and the incongruity of a gin-sopped alien in a 1950s hat.

'The Visitor At The Window' (Travis)

Marshall's echo-bathed rim shots (evoking the original 'Joy Of A Toy' again) form a tantalising bed beneath Travis's alluring flute wound in helixes around Etheridge's sculptural guitar phrases and functioning as a conceptually pleasing reference back to 'Careless Eyes'. It's not until 3:18 that a sax motif arises, and then it's afforded only a couple of iterations – you'll ache for more.

'Maybe Never' (Travis)

Just when you're thinking how much fun it would be to end the album with 'Soft Space'-style disco electronica, we get the next best thing: an interlude of frantic gloops of synth that have their own long heritage through Etheridge's guitar effects and Gong's science fiction landscapes to Ratledge's VCS 3 experiments and a far-off wind-up girl.

'Back In Season' (Travis)

But the actual closer is seven minutes of trippy suspension from its languorous piano introduction to incandescent flute and electric guitar phrases that once more circle each other above the somehow natural-sounding blend of dilatory space rock and elegant jazz that Soft Machine have claimed as their own.

Nektar - *on track*
every album, every song

Scott Meze
Paperback
144 pages
47 colour photographs
978-1-78951-257-0
£15.99
$22.95

**Every album and
every song by these
cult prog legends.**

Of all the British bands that rose to fame in rock's golden age, Nektar remain the most mysterious and least documented. Because they chose to base themselves in West Germany, commentators in their native land tended to overlook them. They're all but excluded from prog's official narrative even though *Remember The Future* is a classic and one of very few European art rock albums to succeed in the USA.

This book reveals Nektar as much more than just a hit LP, celebrating works of equal stature which seemed to pour effortlessly from the players. Whether you know only the 1970s albums that show the band at the pinnacle, or you've followed their progress under leaders Roye Albrighton and now Derek Moore, here is everything you need to complete your understanding of an intriguing band as distinctive as their artwork and as dazzling as their light show.

It documents how Germany was both boon and bane for the band, how America tore them apart and pulled them back together, and how from *Journey To The Centre Of The Eye* to *The Other Side*, Nektar have a vision and a connection that brings them much closer to our lives than any other band of their stature.

Talk Talk - *on track*
every album, every song

Gary Steel
Paperback
144 pages
43 colour photographs
978-1-78951-284-6
£15.99
$22.95

Every album and every song by these cult art rock legends.

In this era of lavish box sets and extravagant vinyl reissues, the sheer economy of Talk Talk's output feels terrific, refreshing and just right. During the group's ten-year lifespan, they released just five studio albums, but in the process, redefined contemporary music and spawned a whole new movement that came to be known as 'post rock', influencing legions of bands in their wake. Leader Mark Hollis's determination to carry out his musical vision would see the group mutate from a synth-pop/new romantic outfit, into the most determinedly unique and unclassifiable art-pop act of the late 20th century. More than 30 years later, the group's astonishing last three albums are still blowing minds and being studiously examined by those who seek to break their mysterious code.

This book examines the whole of Talk Talk's oeuvre song by song, telling their bizarre and somewhat unlikely story along the way as we cast light on the essence of the group through their work. While a book on this compelling band necessarily discusses the tortured genius of singer/guitarist/writer Mark Hollis, it also casts light on the surprising après-Talk Talk careers of foundational members Lee Harris and Paul Webb, as well as that of producer/keyboardist Tim Friese-Greene.

Roy Harper - *on track*
every album, every song

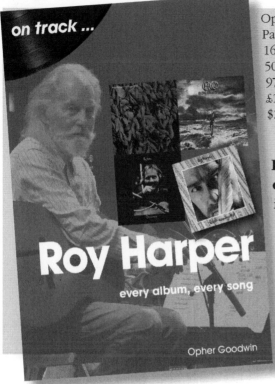

Opher Goodwin
Paperback
160 pages
50 colour photographs
978-1-78951-130-6
£14.99
$21.95

Every album and every song by this influential British singer-songwriter.

Roy Harper must be one of Britain's most undervalued rock musicians and songwriters. For over fifty years, he has produced a series of innovative albums of consistently outstanding quality, putting poetry and social commentary to music in a way that extends the boundaries of rock music. His 22 studio albums and 16 live albums, made up of 250 songs, have created a unique body of work.

Roy is a musician's musician. He is lauded by the likes of Dave Gilmour, Ian Anderson, Jimmy Page, Pete Townsend, Joanna Newsom, Fleet Foxes and Kate Bush. Who else could boast that he has had Keith Moon, Jimmy Page, Dave Gilmour, John Paul Jones, Ronnie Lane, Chris Spedding, Bill Bruford and Steve Broughton in his backing band? Notable albums include *Stormcock*, *HQ* and *Bullinamingvase*.

Opher Goodwin, Roy's friend and a fan, guides the reader through every album and song, providing insight into the recording of the songs as well as the times in which they were recorded. As his loyal and often fanatical fans will attest, Roy has produced a series of epic songs and he remains a raging, uncompromising individual.

On Track series

Allman Brothers Band – Andrew Wild 978-1-78952-252-5
Tori Amos – Lisa Torem 978-1-78952-142-9
Aphex Twin – Beau Waddell 978-1-78952-267-9
Asia – Peter Braidis 978-1-78952-099-6
Badfinger – Robert Day-Webb 978-1-878952-176-4
Barclay James Harvest – Keith and Monica Domone 978-1-78952-067-5
Beck – Arthur Lizie 978-1-78952-258-7
The Beatles – Andrew Wild 978-1-78952-009-5
The Beatles Solo 1969-1980 – Andrew Wild 978-1-78952-030-9
Blue Oyster Cult – Jacob Holm-Lupo 978-1-78952-007-1
Blur – Matt Bishop 978-178952-164-1
Marc Bolan and T.Rex – Peter Gallagher 978-1-78952-124-5
Kate Bush – Bill Thomas 978-1-78952-097-2
Camel – Hamish Kuzminski 978-1-78952-040-8
Captain Beefheart – Opher Goodwin 978-1-78952-235-8
Caravan – Andy Boot 978-1-78952-127-6
Cardiacs – Eric Benac 978-1-78952-131-3
Nick Cave and The Bad Seeds – Dominic Sanderson 978-1-78952-240-2
Eric Clapton Solo – Andrew Wild 978-1-78952-141-2
The Clash – Nick Assirati 978-1-78952-077-4
Elvis Costello and The Attractions – Georg Purvis 978-1-78952-129-0
Crosby, Stills and Nash – Andrew Wild 978-1-78952-039-2
Creedence Clearwater Revival – Tony Thompson 978-178952-237-2
The Damned – Morgan Brown 978-1-78952-136-8
Deep Purple and Rainbow 1968-79 – Steve Pilkington 978-1-78952-002-6
Dire Straits – Andrew Wild 978-1-78952-044-6
The Doors – Tony Thompson 978-1-78952-137-5
Dream Theater – Jordan Blum 978-1-78952-050-7
Eagles – John Van der Kiste 978-1-78952-260-0
Earth, Wind and Fire – Bud Wilkins 978-1-78952-272-3
Electric Light Orchestra – Barry Delve 978-1-78952-152-8
Emerson Lake and Palmer – Mike Goode 978-1-78952-000-2
Fairport Convention – Kevan Furbank 978-1-78952-051-4
Peter Gabriel – Graeme Scarfe 978-1-78952-138-2
Genesis – Stuart MacFarlane 978-1-78952-005-7
Gentle Giant – Gary Steel 978-1-78952-058-3
Gong – Kevan Furbank 978-1-78952-082-8
Green Day – William E. Spevack 978-1-78952-261-7
Hall and Oates – Ian Abrahams 978-1-78952-167-2
Hawkwind – Duncan Harris 978-1-78952-052-1
Peter Hammill – Richard Rees Jones 978-1-78952-163-4
Roy Harper – Opher Goodwin 978-1-78952-130-6

Jimi Hendrix – Emma Stott 978-1-78952-175-7
The Hollies – Andrew Darlington 978-1-78952-159-7
Horslips – Richard James 978-1-78952-263-1
The Human League and The Sheffield Scene –
Andrew Darlington 978-1-78952-186-3
The Incredible String Band – Tim Moon 978-1-78952-107-8
Iron Maiden – Steve Pilkington 978-1-78952-061-3
Joe Jackson – Richard James 978-1-78952-189-4
Jefferson Airplane – Richard Butterworth 978-1-78952-143-6
Jethro Tull – Jordan Blum 978-1-78952-016-3
Elton John in the 1970s – Peter Kearns 978-1-78952-034-7
Billy Joel – Lisa Torem 978-1-78952-183-2
Judas Priest – John Tucker 978-1-78952-018-7
Kansas – Kevin Cummings 978-1-78952-057-6
The Kinks – Martin Hutchinson 978-1-78952-172-6
Korn – Matt Karpe 978-1-78952-153-5
Led Zeppelin – Steve Pilkington 978-1-78952-151-1
Level 42 – Matt Philips 978-1-78952-102-3
Little Feat – Georg Purvis - 978-1-78952-168-9
Aimee Mann – Jez Rowden 978-1-78952-036-1
Joni Mitchell – Peter Kearns 978-1-78952-081-1
The Moody Blues – Geoffrey Feakes 978-1-78952-042-2
Motorhead – Duncan Harris 978-1-78952-173-3
Nektar – Scott Meze – 978-1-78952-257-0
New Order – Dennis Remmer – 978-1-78952-249-5
Nightwish – Simon McMurdo – 978-1-78952-270-9
Laura Nyro – Philip Ward 978-1-78952-182-5
Mike Oldfield – Ryan Yard 978-1-78952-060-6
Opeth – Jordan Blum 978-1-78-952-166-5
Pearl Jam – Ben L. Connor 978-1-78952-188-7
Tom Petty – Richard James 978-1-78952-128-3
Pink Floyd – Richard Butterworth 978-1-78952-242-6
The Police – Pete Braidis 978-1-78952-158-0
Porcupine Tree – Nick Holmes 978-1-78952-144-3
Queen – Andrew Wild 978-1-78952-003-3
Radiohead – William Allen 978-1-78952-149-8
Rancid – Paul Matts 989-1-78952-187-0
Renaissance – David Detmer 978-1-78952-062-0
REO Speedwagon – Jim Romag 978-1-78952-262-4
The Rolling Stones 1963-80 – Steve Pilkington 978-1-78952-017-0
The Smiths and Morrissey – Tommy Gunnarsson 978-1-78952-140-5
Spirit – Rev. Keith A. Gordon – 978-1-78952- 248-8
Stackridge – Alan Draper 978-1-78952-232-7

Status Quo the Frantic Four Years – Richard James 978-1-78952-160-3
Steely Dan – Jez Rowden 978-1-78952-043-9
Steve Hackett – Geoffrey Feakes 978-1-78952-098-9
Tears For Fears – Paul Clark - 978-178952-238-9
Thin Lizzy – Graeme Stroud 978-1-78952-064-4
Tool – Matt Karpe 978-1-78952-234-1
Toto – Jacob Holm-Lupo 978-1-78952-019-4
U2 – Eoghan Lyng 978-1-78952-078-1
UFO – Richard James 978-1-78952-073-6
Van Der Graaf Generator – Dan Coffey 978-1-78952-031-6
Van Halen – Morgan Brown – 9781-78952-256-3
The Who – Geoffrey Feakes 978-1-78952-076-7
Roy Wood and the Move – James R Turner 978-1-78952-008-8
Yes – Stephen Lambe 978-1-78952-001-9
Frank Zappa 1966 to 1979 – Eric Benac 978-1-78952-033-0
Warren Zevon – Peter Gallagher 978-1-78952-170-2
10CC – Peter Kearns 978-1-78952-054-5

Decades Series

The Bee Gees in the 1960s – Andrew Mon Hughes et al 978-1-78952-148-1
The Bee Gees in the 1970s – Andrew Mon Hughes et al 978-1-78952-179-5
Black Sabbath in the 1970s – Chris Sutton 978-1-78952-171-9
Britpop – Peter Richard Adams and Matt Pooler 978-1-78952-169-6
Phil Collins in the 1980s – Andrew Wild 978-1-78952-185-6
Alice Cooper in the 1970s – Chris Sutton 978-1-78952-104-7
Alice Cooper in the 1980s – Chris Sutton 978-1-78952-259-4
Curved Air in the 1970s – Laura Shenton 978-1-78952-069-9
Donovan in the 1960s – Jeff Fitzgerald 978-1-78952-233-4
Bob Dylan in the 1980s – Don Klees 978-1-78952-157-3
Brian Eno in the 1970s – Gary Parsons 978-1-78952-239-6
Faith No More in the 1990s – Matt Karpe 978-1-78952-250-1
Fleetwood Mac in the 1970s – Andrew Wild 978-1-78952-105-4
Fleetwood Mac in the 1980s – Don Klees 978-178952-254-9
Focus in the 1970s – Stephen Lambe 978-1-78952-079-8
Free and Bad Company in the 1970s – John Van der Kiste 978-1-78952-178-8
Genesis in the 1970s – Bill Thomas 978178952-146-7
George Harrison in the 1970s – Eoghan Lyng 978-1-78952-174-0
Kiss in the 1970s – Peter Gallagher 978-1-78952-246-4
Manfred Mann's Earth Band in the 1970s – John Van der Kiste 978178952-243-3
Marillion in the 1980s – Nathaniel Webb 978-1-78952-065-1
Van Morrison in the 1970s – Peter Childs - 978-1-78952-241-9
Mott the Hoople and Ian Hunter in the 1970s –
John Van der Kiste 978-1-78-952-162-7

Pink Floyd In The 1970s – Georg Purvis 978-1-78952-072-9
Suzi Quatro in the 1970s – Darren Johnson 978-1-78952-236-5
Queen in the 1970s – James Griffiths 978-1-78952-265-5
Roxy Music in the 1970s – Dave Thompson 978-1-78952-180-1
Slade in the 1970s – Darren Johnson 978-1-78952-268-6
Status Quo in the 1980s – Greg Harper 978-1-78952-244-0
Tangerine Dream in the 1970s – Stephen Palmer 978-1-78952-161-0
The Sweet in the 1970s – Darren Johnson 978-1-78952-139-9
Uriah Heep in the 1970s – Steve Pilkington 978-1-78952-103-0
Van der Graaf Generator in the 1970s – Steve Pilkington 978-1-78952-245-7
Rick Wakeman in the 1970s – Geoffrey Feakes 978-1-78952-264-8
Yes in the 1980s – Stephen Lambe with David Watkinson 978-1-78952-125-2

On Screen series
Carry On... – Stephen Lambe 978-1-78952-004-0
David Cronenberg – Patrick Chapman 978-1-78952-071-2
Doctor Who: The David Tennant Years – Jamie Hailstone 978-1-78952-066-8
James Bond – Andrew Wild 978-1-78952-010-1
Monty Python – Steve Pilkington 978-1-78952-047-7
Seinfeld Seasons 1 to 5 – Stephen Lambe 978-1-78952-012-5

Other Books
1967: A Year In Psychedelic Rock 978-1-78952-155-9
1970: A Year In Rock – John Van der Kiste 978-1-78952-147-4
1973: The Golden Year of Progressive Rock 978-1-78952-165-8
Babysitting A Band On The Rocks – G.D. Praetorius 978-1-78952-106-1
Eric Clapton Sessions – Andrew Wild 978-1-78952-177-1
Derek Taylor: For Your Radioactive Children –
Andrew Darlington 978-1-78952-038-5
The Golden Road: The Recording History of The Grateful Dead – John Kilbride 978-1-78952-156-6
Iggy and The Stooges On Stage 1967-1974 – Per Nilsen 978-1-78952-101-6
Jon Anderson and the Warriors – the road to Yes –
David Watkinson 978-1-78952-059-0
Magic: The David Paton Story – David Paton 978-1-78952-266-2
Misty: The Music of Johnny Mathis – Jakob Baekgaard 978-1-78952-247-1
Nu Metal: A Definitive Guide – Matt Karpe 978-1-78952-063-7
Tommy Bolin: In and Out of Deep Purple – Laura Shenton 978-1-78952-070-5
Maximum Darkness – Deke Leonard 978-1-78952-048-4
The Twang Dynasty – Deke Leonard 978-1-78952-049-1

and many more to come!

Would you like to write for Sonicbond Publishing?

At Sonicbond Publishing we are always on the look-out for authors, particularly for our two main series:

On Track. Mixing fact with in depth analysis, the On Track series examines the work of a particular musical artist or group. All genres are considered from easy listening and jazz to 60s soul to 90s pop, via rock and metal.

On Screen. This series looks at the world of film and television. Subjects considered include directors, actors and writers, as well as entire television and film series. As with the On Track series, we balance fact with analysis.

While professional writing experience would, of course, be an advantage the most important qualification is to have real enthusiasm and knowledge of your subject. First-time authors are welcomed, but the ability to write well in English is essential.

Sonicbond Publishing has distribution throughout Europe and North America, and all books are also published in E-book form. Authors will be paid a royalty based on sales of their book.

Further details are available from www.sonicbondpublishing.co.uk. To contact us, complete the contact form there or email info@sonicbondpublishing.co.uk